The Paleo Cookbook

ANNA CONRAD

The Paleo Cookbook

90 Grain-Free, Dairy-Free Recipes the Whole Family Will Love

ANNA CONRAD

With special Exercise Section by
DUSTIN MOHR

Skyhorse Publishing

Copyright © 2014 by Anna Conrad
All Rights Reserved. No part of this book may be reproduced in any manner without the express written consent of the publisher, except in the case of brief excerpts in critical reviews or articles. All inquiries should be addressed to Skyhorse Publishing, 307 West 36th Street, 11th Floor, New York, NY 10018.

Skyhorse Publishing books may be purchased in bulk at special discounts for sales promotion, corporate gifts, fund-raising, or educational purposes. Special editions can also be created to specifications. For details, contact the Special Sales Department, Skyhorse Publishing, 307 West 36th Street, 11th Floor, New York, NY 10018or info@skyhorsepublishing.com.

Skyhorse® and Skyhorse Publishing® are registered trademarks of Skyhorse Publishing, Inc.®, a Delaware corporation.

Visit our website at www.skyhorsepublishing.com.

10 9 8 7 6 5 4 3 2 1

Library of Congress Cataloging-in-Publication Data is available on file.
ISBN: 978-1-62636-394-6

Printed in Canada

I'd like to acknowledge the following individuals for their contribution to this book:

John M. Bray, at exposureproductions.net, for photographing the recipes and making them come to life.

Victoria M. Dilliott at wordsrefined.com for helping to make the content of this book more polished and for ensuring the uniformity of the recipe layouts.

Randall Jenkins for coordinating the preparation, testing, and refinement of the recipes.

Chef Anna clients for taste-testing the recipes.

Your help was invaluable, and the book wouldn't be possible without you!

Chef Anna Conrad

{ Contents }

{ Why I Wrote This Book }

Dustin Mohr, the author of the exercise section in this book, introduced me to the paleo diet in 2011. Dustin owns and operates Mohr Fitness in Johnson City, Tennessee, and he asked me to provide one paleo recipe every day for 28 days to a select group of his clients for a 28-day paleo challenge he conducted. Before I agreed, I researched the diet and determined whether or not I was comfortable with the approach. As with any diet I research and consider for promotion, I personally followed the diet for at least two weeks. Needless to say, I was very impressed with the paleo diet.

Below are a few of the reasons why I chose to write this book:

1. The foods are extremely healthy.
2. I was not hungry.
3. I was very satisfied with the food.
4. I lost eight pounds.
5. My blood pressure, heart rate, and cholesterol stayed within healthy limits.

I agreed to provide recipes for Dustin's challenge and decided to provide prepared paleo meals through my personal chef and catering business for the duration of the challenge. Today, the paleo menu continues to be an offering at my business.

{ The Paleolithic Diet in Summary }

The paleo diet was first known as the Paleolithic diet and later shortened to paleo diet. Many refer to the diet as the caveman diet or the Stone Age hunter-gatherer diet. The diet is named after the Paleolithic Era, a period of time that lasted about 2.5 million years and ended about 10,000 years ago. It's widely believed that the first humans lived during the Paleolithic Era and derived their nutrition from a diet based on wild plants and animals. Today's interpretation of the Paleolithic diet consists mainly of meat, fish, vegetables, fruits, and nuts, and excludes grains, legumes, dairy products, salt, refined sugar, and processed oils.

The diet was first popularized in the 1970s by gastroenterologist Walter L. Voegtlin. Since that time, the diet has been adapted by authors and researchers who have detailed the concept in several books and academic journals. There are a growing number of critics and proponents of the diet as it gains popularity in mainstream America and particularly in the athletic community.

While researching this book, I interviewed several medical professionals who believe that of all the low-carbohydrate diets to date, this one has the most merit because its roots are found in the earliest form of human beings before the agricultural, industrial, and information ages tinkered with the food chain.

Proponents of Paleolithic nutrition base their beliefs on the premise that humans are genetically wired to best accept the diet of our Paleolithic ancestors because our genetics have scarcely changed since that time. A central argument for the diet is that many diseases that we suffer from today (and our paleolithic ancestors did not) are "diseases of civilization." They theorize that a diet predating modern agricultural methods might rid humans of such diseases.

{ How Do I Go Paleo? }

Choose the highest-quality ingredients that are available to you, that you can afford to purchase, and that you have time to prepare. Ideal ingredients include:

- Coconut oil and full-fat coconut milk with no added ingredients
- Extra virgin olive oil
- Freshly squeezed juices
- Freshly ground nut butters
- Fresh fruits, herbs, and vegetables
- Freshly ground spices
- Grass-fed fresh meats and poultry that are not injected with solutions or flavorings
- Pure sea salt
- Wild-caught fish without artificial additives
- Organic vegetables, fruits, nuts, and seeds

Take an inventory of your refrigerator and freezer. Those items not on the "green light" or "yellow light" lists on pages xvii–xxiv should be donated to a local food bank—no exceptions. If you keep them in the house, you are likely to eat them. No, you shouldn't keep them for the kids. Remember, if you think this diet is healthy for you and you shouldn't be eating chips and cookies, then it's true for your children, too!

On Saturday or Sunday, look through the recipe section of this book and choose which recipes you will make for the following week. Create a grocery list and go shopping. Make sure you eat before shopping, so that you aren't tempted to purchase something not on your list of approved foods.

{ The Truth About Fat }

Medical authorities have long held it true that consumption of saturated animal fat is unhealthy and causes heart disease.

But only 100 years ago there were fewer than 1 in 100 obese Americans. Coronary heart disease wasn't even a medical term in those days. We started seeing coronary heart disease when companies introduced trans fats in products like margarine, shortening, and partially hydrogenated oil.

Shortening-like products were originally used to make soap and candles, but with the increasing use of electric lights, candles sales were on the decline. So the companies that sold those original trans fats made a decision to market them as a healthier fat derived from vegetables and fit for human consumption.

They may not have known at the time the impact that trans fats would have on the human heart. Now, research shows that *trans fats* are the biggest problem when it comes to heart disease, *not* saturated fats as a whole.

In 1953, Dr. Ansell Keyes conducted the first studies that indicated saturated fats were unhealthy. He studied six countries in which higher saturated fat intake equated to higher rates of coronary heart disease. He omitted data from sixteen other countries that did not indicate the same findings. Had he included the historical data from these other sixteen countries, he would have seen that saturated fat had no linkage to coronary heart disease. The populations of those countries consumed high levels of saturated fats and were actually very healthy.

The work done by Dr. Keyes led to a low-fat craze of dieting in the United States. Today, we are beginning to see that fats can be good as long as you eat the right ones. Low-fat diets leave you hungry and unsatisfied. Most of them depend on high levels of carbo-hydrates for your body's energy needs. After decades of consuming low-fat products, we are seeing the results: gluten intolerance, obesity, and other disorders like type 2 diabetes. Coronary heart disease continues to be a problem and is, in fact, on the rise.

It's time to take a more balanced look at how we eat. Only healthy carbohydrates from natural sources like fruits and vegetables and lean proteins should be included in our diet. Healthy fats like those derived from olives, coconuts, avocados, palm oil, safflower oil and sunflower oil, animal fats, nuts, and eggs are the sorts of fats that *should* be included in our diet. These healthy fats are the foundation of the paleo diet.

Saturated fats from animal and vegetable sources are critical to the performance of many of our bodily functions. Eat good fats to support the healthy functioning of your cell membranes, liver, immune system, heart, lungs, bones, and hormones.

{ Healthy Fats }

Coconut oil

Coconut oil is the primary fat for most paleo dieters. In fact, paleo dieters eat every part of the coconut because there are so many positive health benefits.

Coconut oil is greater than 90% saturated fat, making it very stable at room temperature. Virgin coconut oil has a subtle, wonderful flavor that will enhance almost any dish.

Coconut oil contains a large percentage of lauric acid, a medium-chain fatty acid that is easy to digest. This fatty acid is said to have antimicrobial and antifungal properties, which is one more benefit to using it regularly in cooking and baking.

Animal fats

Animal fats are a key source of energy and critical to healthy body function on the paleo diet. Cavemen ate animals regularly, consuming a lot of natural fat from animal sources.

Animal fats have two interesting properties that make them desirable for use in cooking: They are highly saturated, which lends to their heat stability at high temperatures, and they are solid at room temperature, so they do not need to be refrigerated. A third added benefit is that they are usually inexpensive to purchase.

Animal fats can be purchased from your local butcher. Ask for duck fat, beef tallow, or pork fat. They may not have the fat already rendered, but that is easy enough to do yourself.

Rendering animal fat

Use a slow cooker or a heavy-bottomed Dutch oven to render the fat. Using a sharp knife, remove any meat or veins from the fat. Rinse the fat under cold water to remove any blood, and cut the fat into chunks. Place the chunks in your slow cooker or Dutch oven. Cook over very low heat until all of the white fat turns brown.

Strain the fat and allow it to cool to room temperature. You will notice that the fat is white again. Store it at room temperature in a container with a tight-fitting lid. Use as needed in recipes that call for high-temperature cooking.

Olive oil

Olive oil is a vegetable oil that is mostly monounsaturated fat. It is healthy and safe, not to mention delicious! Olive oil should only be used to cook at very low temperatures, or it can oxidize and create compounds that are unhealthy for humans. Use olive oil primarily in dressings or for drizzling on top of cooked foods. I like to use a good extra virgin olive oil topping on many of my dishes.

Olive oils are light sensitive—therefore, you should purchase them in dark bottles, which haven't been on the shelf for a long time. Once you get the oil home, store in a dark, cool place (a cupboard or the refrigerator) to extend the shelf life. It will become cloudy and thick in the refrigerator, but will return to its original fluidity and appearance after it comes to room temperature.

Avocados and avocado oil

Avocados are one of the only fatty fruits. They are rich in B vitamins, potassium, vitamin E, and fiber. Avocados are wonderful sliced and served as a side or on salads. Don't forget guacamole–one of my favorite versatile sides.

Other fat sources

You can get fats from other sources, too, including eggs, nuts, and nut butters. Just remember to eat nuts and nut butters in moderation. They contain high levels of omega-6 fatty acids, which can trigger an allergic reaction in some people. Start with a small amount, see how your body reacts, and then go from there. When choosing oils, experiment and see what works for you!

{ Food Do's and Don'ts }

In its purest form, the theory of the paleo diet states that if your ancestors didn't eat it, you shouldn't either. On the other hand, some foods that our ancestors did not eat are known to be very nutritious. For example, beans are a great source of numerous nutrients, and dairy products can be a great source of calcium and protein. Some experts urge that a slightly less strict, slightly more moderate form of the paleo diet should be followed for optimal health. Everyone is different; you will need to decide how to best fit this diet into your own life.

Many of the recipes in this book use coconut oil because that's the cooking fat of choice for most paleo dieters. But you can substitute any approved fat for the coconut oil in most recipes.

When approaching food for the paleo diet, think about them as you would approach a traffic signal: green, yellow or red light.

Green Light foods: Foods that you may eat without restriction.

Yellow Light foods: Foods you should approach with caution and consume in moderation.

Red Light foods: Foods you should avoid because, in all likelihood, they were not available to our paleo ancestors.

{ Green Light Foods }

Certain foods are encouraged on the paleo diet because they support its principles and closely match what our ancestors might have consumed. Boredom with food is one of the top reasons why people abandon a diet. Eat a variety of meats, fish, poultry, eggs, vegetables, fruits, and nuts to keep the diet interesting!

Lean meats

Lean cuts of meat are a great way to get protein into your diet and keep you feeling full and satisfied. I prefer to eat meats from grass-fed animals because that's what our ancestors would have eaten. Listed below are several examples of lean meats. But, don't let this limit you; feel free to prepare lean meat of all kinds and use grass-fed versions as often as possible for maximum benefits:

- Lean beef (trimmed of visible fat): flank steak, top sirloin steak, extra-lean hamburger (no more than 7% fat, extra fat drained off after cooking), London broil, chuck steak, and lean veal
- Lean pork (trimmed of visible fat): pork tenderloin and pork chops
- Rabbit meat (any cut)
- Goat meat (any cut)

Organ meats

Organ meats are one of the most nutrient-dense foods available, rich with vitamins, minerals, amino acids, and other nutrients. Our ancestors knew the value of organ meats. For example, look at the nutrients contained in beef kidneys:

Nutrients in 4 ounces of raw beef kidney:

Calories: 121, protein: 18.7 g, carbohydrates: 2.45 g, total fat: 3.5 g, fiber: 0.0 g, iron (8.3 mg), vitamin B12 (30.5 mcg), vitamin A (994 IU), and folate (90.4 mcg)

Below are the organ meats commonly recognized as acceptable for the paleo diet because they would have been available to our paleo ancestors:

- Beef, lamb, pork, and chicken livers
- Beef, pork, and lamb tongues
- Beef, lamb, and pork marrow
- Beef, lamb, and pork sweetbreads

Game meat

Whether you purchase them at the grocery store or hunt them as our ancestors did, game meats are a delicious and nutritious addition to any menu.

Below are the game meats commonly recognized as acceptable for the paleo diet because they would have been available to our paleo ancestors. But, don't this list stop you from considering other lean game meats:

- Alligator
- Bear
- Bison (buffalo)
- Caribou, elk, and reindeer
- Emu and ostrich
- Goose, Muscovy duck, and quail
- Kangaroo
- Venison and New Zealand Cervena® deer
- Rattlesnake
- Squab
- Turtle
- Wild boar
- Wild turkey

Poultry

Poultry meat is not only tasty, easy to prepare, and appropriate for different food combinations, but it is also a natural source of vitamins, minerals, proteins, and healthy fats. To qualify as lean poultry, it should have the skin removed and be white meat only. Consider the following poultry when planning your paleo menu, and use grass-fed poultry whenever possible:

- Chicken breast
- Turkey breast
- Game hen breast
- Any other white meat from poultry

Eggs

All natural, high-quality protein such as that found in eggs is a great way to provide active adults and children with the energy needed on their busiest days.

Below are the eggs commonly recognized as acceptable for the paleo diet because they would have been available to our paleo ancestors:

- Chicken
- Duck
- Goose

Fish and shellfish

Eating the fish and shellfish listed on our encouraged foods list is an extremely efficient and healthy way to gain high-quality proteins with the right amount of amino acids needed for healthy bodily function. The fats in fish and shellfish are predominantly omega-3 fatty acids, and fish oil is also a natural source of vitamin D.

Below are the fish commonly recognized as acceptable for the paleo diet because they would have been available to our paleo ancestors:

- Bass
- Bluefish
- Cod
- Drum
- Eel
- Flatfish
- Grouper
- Haddock
- Halibut
- Herring
- Mackerel
- Monkfish
- Mullet
- Northern pike
- Orange roughy
- Perch
- Red snapper
- Rockfish
- Salmon
- Scrod
- Shark
- Striped bass
- Sunfish
- Tilapia
- Trout
- Tuna
- Turbot
- Walleye
- Any other commercially available wildcaught fish

Below are the shellfish commonly recognized as acceptable for the paleo diet because they would have been available to our paleo ancestors:

- Abalone
- Clams
- Crab
- Crayfish
- Lobster
- Mussels
- Oysters
- Scallops
- Shrimp

Vegetables and fruits

Diets rich in vegetables help lower blood pressure, can reduce the risk of heart disease, and possibly some cancers, and can promote good eye and digestive system health. Vegetables also help us control our blood sugar and, as a result, our appetite.

You should eat at least nine paleo-encouraged vegetables and fruits each day (about 4 ½ cups total). Choose a variety of types and colors. The darker green, red, orange, or yellow, the better they are for you.

Fruits and vegetables can be great sources of the nutrients important for building healthy bones, decreasing coronary heart disease, reducing brain and spinal cord defects, and encouraging healthy blood and functioning of cells. They also contribute to healthy blood pressure, healthy teeth and gums, healing of cuts and wounds, and healthy eyes and skin.

Below are some green light vegetables:

- Artichokes
- Asparagus
- Beets and beet greens
- Bell peppers (all colors)
- Broccoli
- Brussels sprouts
- Cabbage (any color)
- Carrots and parsnips
- Cauliflower
- Celery
- Cucumbers
- Dandelion greens
- Eggplant
- Endives
- Green onions, onions, and chives
- Kale, mustard greens, Swiss chard, and collard greens
- Kohlrabi
- Lettuce (all varieties)
- Mushrooms
- Parsley
- Peppers (hot and sweet, all kinds)
- Pumpkins and all varieties of squash
- Purslane
- Radishes
- Rutabaga
- Seaweed
- Spinach
- Rhubarb
- Tomatillos and tomatoes (actually a fruit, but most people think of it as a vegetable)
- Turnips and turnip greens
- Watercress

Below are the fruits commonly recognized as acceptable for the paleo diet:

- Apples
- Apricots
- Avocados
- Bananas
- All berries, including but not limited to blackberry, blueberry, boysenberry, cranberry, gooseberry, strawberry, and raspberry
- All melons, including cantaloupe, casaba melon, honeydew melon, and watermelon
- Carambolas
- Cherimoyas
- Cherries
- Figs
- Grapefruits
- Grapes
- Guavas
- Kiwis
- All citrus fruits, including lemon**and lime**, orange, and pineapple
- Lychees
- Mangoes
- Nectarine and peachs
- Papayas
- Passion fruits
- Pears
- Persimmons
- Plums
- Pomegranates
- Star fruits
- All other fruits

**Note: The juice of one medium lemon is approximately 2 to 3 Tbsp. The juice of one medium lime is approximately 2 Tbsp. It is important that you use a fresh lemon or lime to get the juice if you are following the diet properly.

Nuts and seeds

Many nuts and seeds include the nutrients magnesium, manganese, protein, fiber, zinc and phosphorus. Raw nuts are naturally cholesterol-free and only contain traces of sodium.

Below are the nuts recommended for the paleo diet:

- Almonds
- Cashews
- Pecans
- Hazelnuts
- Filberts

{ Yellow Light Foods }

The following foods are acceptable to eat in moderation. But, if you minimize their use, you will be able to control your weight better.

Oils and fats

Consume no more than 4 Tbsp each day if your goal is to lose or maintain your weight.

Acceptable fats include:

- Coconut oil
- Animal tallow
- Olive oil
- Avocado oil

Poultry

Acceptable poultry meats include:

- Whole chicken
- Whole turkey
- Whole game hens

Fatty meats

Our paleo ancestors may have eaten these, but their diet was calorically restricted whereas ours are not. Today, there is no need for most of us to consume extra fat in order to get the necessary calories needed for energy each day.

Acceptable fatty meats include:

- Bacon (with no artificial ingredients)
- Fatty beef roasts and other fatty cuts of beef
- Beef ribs
- Fatty ground beef
- T-bone steaks
- Poultry thighs, skin, legs, or wings
- Fatty pork chops and roasts
- Pork ribs
- Pork sausage (with no artificial ingredients)
- Lamb chops and roasts
- Leg of lamb

Starchy vegetables

There is some disagreement amongst paleo dieters as to whether or not starchy vegetables were available and used by our ancestors as a source of carbohydrates in their diet. For this reason, I'm including them in the Yellow Light foods section, so that you will be careful with their consumption and only eat as much of them as necessary. In general, athletes and people with an active lifestyle need more of these starchy vegetables than people who are attempting to lose weight. Children who are still growing may also need a few more carbohydrates than adults. Caution: Adding starchy carbohydrates to your diet will increase appetite and create a psychological response to eat more starch than you need, so proceed with caution!

- Starchy tubers
- Sweet potatoes
- Cassava root
- Yams
- Tapioca products
- Manioc
- White potatoes
- Sweet potatoes
- Lotus root
- Carrots
- Jicama

Nuts and seeds

Do not consume more than four ounces of these nuts per day.

Acceptable nuts and seeds include:

- Pine nuts
- Pumpkin seeds
- Sunflower seeds
- Brazil nuts
- Chestnuts
- Macadamia nuts
- Pistachios (unsalted)
- Sesame seeds
- Walnuts

Beverages

When drinking a standard-size mixed drink, glass of wine or beer, women absorb twice as much alcohol into the bloodstream as compared with men. Women typically have a higher proportion of body fat than men and, because fat does not absorb alcohol, more alcohol goes directly into a woman's bloodstream. Women also lack dehydrogenase, an enzyme, that breaks down alcohol in the stomach. Because of these differences, men, on average, can consume twice as much alcohol as women and still be within the limits of healthy consumption of these Yellow Light beverages.

Asians and Native Americans lack the enzyme necessary for the liver to detoxify alcohol and should consider avoiding alcoholic drinks altogether.

Acceptable beverages include:

- Diet sodas
- Beer (24-ounce maximum for men and 12-ounce maximum for women)
- Coffee
- Tea
- Alcohol, such as whiskey, scotch, vodka, tequila, etc., without mixers added (limit 4 ounces per day)
- Wine (8-ounce maximum for men and 4-ounce maximum for women)

Dried fruits

Paleo dieters should consume no more than 2 ounces of unsweetened dried fruit and with no artificial ingredients added per day.

Acceptable dried fruits include, but are not limited to:

- Banana
- Papaya
- Pineapple
- Apple
- Apricot
- Mango
- Cherry
- Cranberry
- Grape
- Plum
- Dates

{ Red Light Foods }

Dairy products

Most dairy products were not available for consumption by our paleo ancestors and should be avoided.

Red Light dairy products are all processed foods made with dairy:

- Powdered milk
- Ice cream
- Butter
- Cheese
- Non-fat dairy creamer

Skim, whole, and low-fat milk

- Frozen yogurt
- Ice milk
- Yogurt
- Heavy cream and half & half
- Dairy spreads (including cream cheese)

Cereal grains

Cereal grains were not available for consumption by our paleo ancestors.

Red light grains include:

- Barley (including barley soup, barley bread, and all processed foods made with barley)
- Corn (corn on and off the cob, corn tortillas, corn chips, cornstarch, corn syrup)
- Millet
- Oats (steel-cut oats, rolled oats, and all processed foods made with oats)
- Rice (brown rice, white rice, wild rice, top ramen, rice noodles, basmati rice, rice cakes, rice flour, and all processed foods made with rice)
- Rye (rye bread, rye crackers, and all processed foods made with rye)
- Sorghum
- Wheat (bread, rolls, muffins, noodles, crackers, cookies, cake, doughnuts, pancakes, waffles, all pasta, wheat tortillas, pizza crust, pita bread, flat bread, and all processed foods made with wheat or wheat flour)

Seeds

These seeds are similar to cereal grains and should not be consumed on the paleo diet:

- Amaranth
- Buckwheat
- Quinoa

Legumes

Though it's hard to know for sure, we assume that legumes were not available for consumption by our paleo ancestors.

Red light legumes include:

- All beans (adzuki beans, black beans, broad beans, fava beans, field beans, garbanzo beans, horse beans, kidney beans, lima beans, mung beans, navy beans, pinto beans, red beans, string beans, white beans including great northern, navy and cannellini)
- Black eyed peas
- Chickpeas
- Peanuts (including peanut butter)
- Lentils
- All peas (snow peas, green peas, and sugar snap peas)
- Miso
- Soybeans and all soybean products (including tofu)

Industrially processed, high sodium foods

Obviously, processed foods were not available for consumption by our paleo ancestors.

Red light processed foods include:

- Bacon that contains artificial ingredients
- Processed meats (including pork rinds, salami, deli meats, frankfurters and hot dogs, sausages with artificial ingredients, and pepperoni)
- Processed cheese
- Ketchup and other commercially processed condiments
- Pickled foods
- Olives
- Salted nuts
- Salted spices
- Smoked, dried and salted fish, or meat containing artificial ingredients
- Canned meats or fish

Soft drinks and fruit juices

Our paleo ancestors didn't have these sweet, processed beverages, and neither should you:

- All regular soft drinks
- Juices or beverages of any kind sweetened with industrially processed sugars or sweeteners

Sweets

These were not available for consumption by our paleo ancestors:

- Candy
- Industrially processed syrups
- Refined sugars
- Industrially processed honey
- Industrially processed sweeteners of any kind

{ 28-Day Challenge }

Sometimes we need a little push to try something new. Challenge yourself to try the paleo diet for 28 days. To make it easier, we've included a twenty-eight day meal plan using recipes found in this book.

If you don't want to prepare a new recipe for each meal for 28 days, use a blank template (or one of the ones provided in the back of the book) to create your own meal plan. Consider making an extra serving of some of the recipes, so that you can have leftovers for breakfast, lunch, or dinner another day during the week.

Now what are you waiting for? Go Paleo!

28-Day Challenge-Weeks 1 and 2 Menus

Day	Week 1	Week 2
Mon	B: Protein Fruit Smoothie L: Zesty Scallop Salad D: Curry Chicken	B: Eggs Over Greens L: Baby Greens and Shrimp D: Beef Heart Stir-Fry
Tue	B: Pumpkin Spice Pancakes L: Broccoli Salad D: Zingy Pulled Pork	B: Protein Fruit Smoothie L: Lamb Leg Soup D: Pork Tenderloin with Fruit and Onions
Wed	B: Seafood Omelet L: Mushroom Stew D: Minted Beef Stir-Fry	B: Italian Omelet L: Chicken & Zucchini Salad D: Nut-Crusted Salmon
Thu	B: Pumpkin Spice Muffins L: Tossed Salad with Orange and Rosemary Vinaigrette D: Traditional Meatloaf	B: Almond Butter "Oatmeal" L: Waldorf Chicken Salad D: Spicy Barbecue Shrimp
Fri	B: Almond Butter "Oatmeal" L: Ratatouille D: Garlic Lime Chicken	B: Pumpkin Spice Pancakes L: Bison Chili D: Sausage Pizza

28-Day Challenge-Weeks 1 and 2 Menus (Continued)

Day	Week 1	Week 2
Sat	B: Italian Omelet L: Turkey Burgers D: Lemon Dill Trout	B: Protein Fruit Smoothie L: Stuffed Portobello D:"Butter" Chicken
Sun	B: Protein Fruit Smoothie L: Fajitas D: "Spaghetti" with Meat Sauce	B: Banana Raisin Muffins L: Citrus and Spinach Beef Stir-Fry D: Hot Cilantro Shrimp

28-Day Challenge-Weeks 3 and 4 Menus

Day	Week 3	Week 4
Mon	B: Protein Fruit Smoothie L: Baba Ghanoush D: Goulash	B: Eggs Over Greens L: Basil Pesto Chicken Stir-Fry D: Poultry and Oranges Stir-Fry
Tue	B: Pumpkin Spice Pancakes L: Salad with Caesar Dressing D: Curry Chicken	B: Protein Fruit Smoothie L: Citrus Shrimp Stir-Fry D: Cilantro Pork Stir-Fry
Wed	B: Seafood Omelet L: Lime and Garlic Scallops D: Spicy Chicken with Spinach Herb Sauce	B: Italian Omelet L: Butternut Squash Soup D: Ginger Lime Chicken
Thu	B: Pumpkin Spice Muffins L: Baked Fish with Asparagus and Roasted Beets D: Steak and Eggs	B: Almond Butter "Oatmeal" L: Waldorf Chicken Salad D: Spicy Barbecue Shrimp
Fri	B: Almond Butter "Oatmeal" L: Red Cabbage and Apple Stir-Fry D: Liver and Onions	B: Pumpkin Spice Pancakes L: Bison Chili D: Traditional Meatloaf
Sat	B: Grab-N-Go Egg Muffins L: Turkey Burgers D: White Balsamic Mussels	B: Protein Fruit Smoothie L: Tossed Salad with Balsamic Vinaigrette D: Oxtail Vihannes
Sun	B: Protein Fruit Smoothie L: Egg Stir-Fry D: Pork Tenderloin with Fruit and Onions	B: Banana Raisin Muffins L: Veggie Kebabs D: Basil Salmon with Coconut Cream Sauce

{ Recipe Index }

{ Breakfast }

Pumpkin Spice Pancakes

SERVES 2

Ingredients

1½ cups almond flour

½ tsp baking soda

¼ tsp sea salt

½ tsp pumpkin pie spice

3 large eggs, at room temperature

2 Tbsp agave nectar or honey

1 tsp vanilla extract

Maple syrup, for serving

5 Tbsp coconut oil, melted and cooled slightly

Preparation

1. Combine all dry ingredients in bowl. Combine egg, nectar or honey, and vanilla in separate bowl and whisk in melted oil.

2. Fold wet ingredients into dry ones and mix well to combine. Batter will appear a little thicker than normal pancake mix.

3. Drop ¼ cup-size dollops of batter onto lightly oiled, non-stick frying pan over medium heat. You might want to shape pancakes with scoop to keep them from being too thick.

4. Flip pancake when bubbles start forming on top.

5. Once slightly browned on both sides, slide pancakes onto plates and serve warm with all-natural maple syrup.

Almond Butter "Oatmeal"

Ingredients

6 Tbsp organic unsweetened applesauce

2 Tbsp raw, chunky almond butter

1 to 2 Tbsp unsweetened coconut milk

Cinnamon to taste

Preparation

1. Combine all ingredients in saucepan on stove over medium-high heat until very warm, stirring constantly.
2. If mixture is too thick, add more coconut milk to achieve desired consistency. Serve warm in bowl, with fresh berries, if desired.

Banana Raisin Muffins

SERVES 4–6

Ingredients

2 cups blanched almond flour

2 tsp baking soda

1 tsp sea salt

1 Tbsp cinnamon

1 cup raisins

3 medium bananas, ripe

3 large eggs

1 tsp apple cider vinegar

¼ cup coconut oil, melted and slightly cooled

1½ cups carrots, grated

¾ cup pecans, finely chopped

¼ cup coconut oil, for greasing muffin tins

Preparation

1. Soak raisins in enough warm water that they are completely covered. When plump, pour off water and continue with preparation.
2. Combine flour, baking soda, salt, and cinnamon in bowl. Whisk to combine.
3. In food processor, combine raisins, bananas, eggs, vinegar, and the melted coconut oil, and process until mostly smooth.
4. Transfer banana mixture to large bowl.
5. Add the dry mix to banana mixture and stir to combine. Fold in carrots and pecans.
6. Grease each muffin cup generously with coconut oil to keep muffins from sticking. Spoon muffin mixture into tins, filling them ½ to ¾ of the way to the top.
7. Bake at 350° for 25 minutes, or until a toothpick comes out clean when inserted in center of muffin. Allow to cool for at least 10 minutes before removing from pan.

Pumpkin Spice Muffins

SERVES 4–6

Ingredients

1½ cups almond flour

3 large eggs

1 tsp baking powder

1 tsp baking soda

⅛ tsp salt

1 tsp ground cinnamon

¾ cup pumpkin puree, unsweetened

½ tsp vanilla extract

⅛ tsp almond extract

1 medium banana, mashed

2 tsp coconut oil, melted

⅛ cup sliced almonds, for garnish

¼ cup coconut oil, for greasing tins

Preparation

1. Mix almond flour, baking powder, soda, salt, and cinnamon in bowl. Whisk to combine.
2. Mix pumpkin, vanilla extract, almond extract, eggs, mashed banana, and melted coconut oil in separate bowl. Stir well to combine. Add wet ingredients to dry ingredients and mix well.
3. Grease 6 muffin tins with coconut oil, and spoon mixture into muffin tins, filling them ½ to ¾ of the way full.
4. Bake at 350° F for 25 minutes, or until toothpick comes out clean when inserted in center of muffin.
5. Press sliced almond on top of muffins during the last 10 minutes of baking.

Italian Omelet

Ingredients

4 large eggs

1 Tbsp olive oil

1 tsp dried oregano or basil

¼ cup onion, chopped

¼ cup bell peppers, chopped

¼ cup tomatoes, chopped

1 cup baby spinach leaves, chopped

4 oz cooked lean meat of choice, diced

Sea salt and black pepper, to taste

Preparation

1. Crack eggs into a medium bowl. Add oregano or basil, salt, and pepper, and whisk.
2. Coat non-stick skillet with olive oil. Pour half of egg mixture into skillet. Cook over medium heat for 1–2 minutes. Tilt pan and lift edges of omelet with a fork to allow runny egg to flow under cooked regions.
3. Once eggs have begun to set, sprinkle half of chopped vegetables and diced meat over one side of eggs.
4. Using spatula, fold empty half of egg mixture over meat and vegetables. Cook for 1 minute more. Using spatula, remove omelet from skillet and keep it warm while you make other omelet.
5. Serve omelets garnished with fresh herbs, if desired.

Grab-N-Go Egg Muffins

SERVES 2

Ingredients

4 large eggs

⅛ cup cooked lean meat, diced

⅛ cup bell pepper, diced

⅛ cup onion, diced

⅛ cup broccoli, cut into small pieces

⅛ cup asparagus, chopped

Sea salt and black pepper, to taste

⅛ cup mayonnaise (page 211)

4 tsp coconut oil, for greasing tins

Preparation

1. Preheat oven to 350° F.
2. Place eggs in bowl and whisk. Add diced meat, vegetables, sea salt, ground pepper, and mayonnaise. Stir to combine.
3. Grease each muffin cup with about 1 tsp of coconut oil. Pour egg mixture into muffin tin.
4. Bake egg muffins for 10–15 minutes, or until egg is set and no longer jiggles in center.
5. Remove from oven and cool on rack for 3 minutes. Using butter knife, gently remove muffins from tins, and serve warm.

Increase the recipe to have muffins to eat for multiple days. Just store them in the refrigerator for up to 5 days and reheat in the microwave for 15–20 seconds on high before serving. These are a great grab and go snack.

Seafood Omelet

Ingredients

---

4 large eggs, beaten

Sea salt and ground black pepper, to taste

½ medium Roma tomato, diced

½ medium ripe avocado, peeled, seeded, and diced

1 tsp ground coriander

1 Tbsp olive oil

1 cup cooked shrimp, scallops, fish, lobster, or seafood of choice, chopped

---

Preparation

1. Add eggs, sea salt, and black pepper to bowl. Whisk until fluffy.
2. In separate bowl, toss diced tomato and avocado with coriander and set aside.
3. Over medium-high heat, heat oil in 8-inch non-stick skillet. Pour eggs into hot skillet, tilting and shaking pan gently. Lift edges of omelet with spatula to allow runny egg to reach sides and flow under cooked egg. Repeat until eggs just begin to set.
4. Spread chopped seafood over center third of omelet. Using spatula, fold each side of omelet over food in center section. Tilt pan to roll omelet into cylindrical shape. Cook 20 seconds longer, careful not to brown egg (unless you like it that way).
5. Slide omelet onto plate or use spatula to remove it to a plate. Top with avocado and tomato mixture.

Eggs Over Greens

Ingredients

½ cup mustard greens, chopped
½ cup chard, chopped
¼ medium onion, diced
1 garlic clove, minced
1½ Tbsp coconut oil (for greens)
1 tsp coconut oil (for eggs)
4 large eggs
1 medium avocado, peeled, seeded and sliced

Preparation

1. Add the coconut oil for the greens to a non-stick pan and melt over medium heat. Add mustard greens, chard, onion, and garlic to the skillet and sauté until greens are tender. Remove everything from the skillet, leaving the juices behind. Place mixture on a plate and set aside and keep warm.
2. Add the coconut oil for the eggs to the juices in the hot skillet. Add eggs to the skillet, careful not to break the yolks, and cook over easy.
3. Place cooked eggs on top of greens mixture and top eggs with sliced avocado. Serve immediately.

Egg Salad

Ingredients

2 Tbsp coconut oil, melted and cooled slightly

1 medium onion, finely diced

1 lb button mushrooms, finely chopped

8 large eggs

Freshly ground black pepper, to taste

Sea salt, to taste

Preparation

1. Place whole eggs in bottom of pot, cover with water and place on stove over high heat. Cover pot with lid and bring to a boil. Reduce heat to medium-high (at a setting that water will maintain a gentle boil) for 9 minutes.

2. Remove eggs from pot with slotted spoon and place in large bowl of ice water (enough to cover eggs). Allow eggs to cool until you can handle them comfortably.

3. Meanwhile, add coconut oil to non-stick skillet over medium heat. Once the oil is melted, add onion and sea salt, and sauté until onion is translucent, 5–6 minutes. Add button mushrooms and sauté another 5 minutes, or until mushrooms are tender and slightly darkened. Remove the skillet from heat and set aside to cool.

4. Lightly tap cooled eggs on countertop to crack shell. Gently peel away shell, careful not to peel away egg with it. Repeat for all eggs. Using plastic cutting board, chop eggs and place in bowl.

5. Toss chopped eggs with pepper and mixture from skillet. Cover and store in refrigerator until chilled. Serve cold.

Protein Fruit Smoothie

SERVES 1

Ingredients

---

15 oz coconut milk (about one can), cold

1 cup fruit (choose something in season or use frozen fruit without additives)

1 or 2 raw eggs (for added fat and protein, optional)

2 tsp nut butter of choice

⅛ tsp vanilla or almond extract

Sea salt, to taste

Preparation

1. Place all ingredients in blender or smoothie maker. Blend until creamy. Serve cold.

{ **Soups and Stews** }

Mushroom Stew

SERVES 4

Ingredients

1 lb cremini mushrooms, or a variety of mushrooms

2 Tbsp coconut oil

½ cup onion, chopped

4 garlic cloves, minced

½ cup beef stock (page 243)

15 oz coconut milk (about one can)

1 handful of fresh thyme, leaves picked from stems, or 1 Tbsp dried thyme

1 medium green onion, thinly sliced

Sea salt and freshly ground black pepper, to taste

Preparation

1. Remove tough portions of stems from mushrooms and discard. Moisten cloth or paper towel and gently scrub mushrooms to remove any dirt or debris. Chop mushrooms and set aside.

2. Heat coconut oil in large, deep non-stick skillet over medium heat until it has melted.

3. Add onions to skillet and sauté until translucent, 5–7 minutes. Add minced garlic and cook for another 30 seconds.

4. Add mushrooms to skillet and season to taste with salt and pepper. Cook for 5–10 minutes or until mushrooms are tender, darkened, and moisture from them has evaporated.

5. Add meat stock and coconut milk to skillet, and stir until well combined. Reduce heat and simmer for 5 minutes.

6. Add thyme leaves and green onions to skillet. Stir and taste. Add more salt and pepper, if desired. Continue simmering until slightly thickened.

7. Serve warm.

Lamb Leg Stew

SERVES 8

Ingredients

1½ lbs lamb leg

2 Tbsp coconut oil

2 medium onions, coarsely chopped

½ lb button mushrooms, sliced (optional)

2 medium carrots, sliced

10 whole black peppercorns

2 large sprigs thyme

1 bay leaf

8 cups beef or lamb stock (page 243)

Sea salt and freshly ground black pepper, to taste

1½ Tbsp lime or lemon juice

Preparation

1. Trim visible fat from lamb, leaving small amount, if desired. Cut lamb into bite-sized pieces.
2. Heat non-stick pot or Dutch oven over medium-high heat and add half the coconut oil. When skillet is hot, add onions and mushrooms (if using) and cook, stirring occasionally, until onion is soft—about 6 minutes.
3. Add lamb pieces and cook, stirring occasionally, until lamb is browned on surface but pink in center (medium rare).
4. While lamb is browning, make sachet bag of cheesecloth and put whole peppercorns, thyme springs, and bay leaf inside it, tying it shut with butcher's twine.
5. Pour stock into pot with lamb, and add sachet of spices and herbs.
6. Bring to a boil, and then reduce to a simmer and cook, covered, for about 2 hours. Add carrots and continue simmering for 30–45 minutes, or until carrots are tender but not mushy.
7. Discard sachet of herbs and spices, add lime or lemon juice to taste, stir, and serve warm.

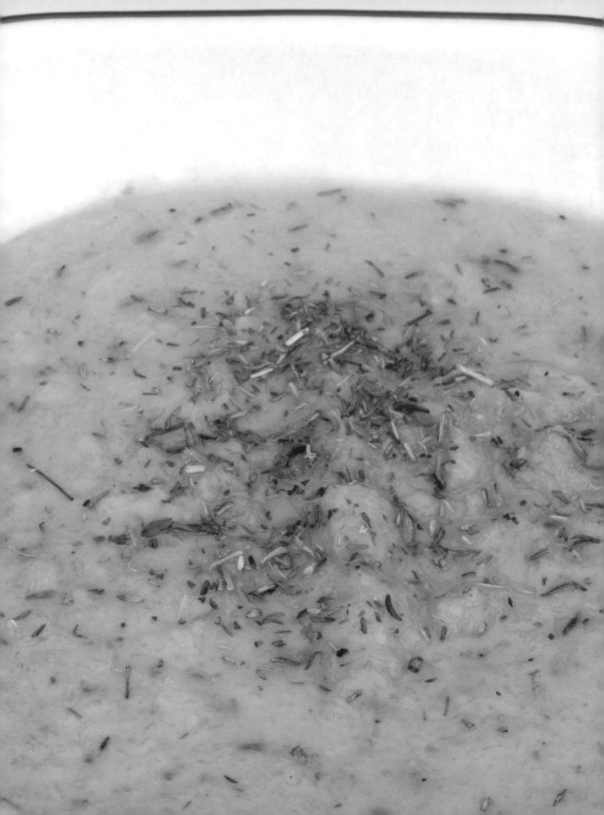

Butternut Squash Soup

Ingredients

---

1 medium butternut squash
15 oz coconut milk
Sea salt and freshly ground black pepper, to taste
Fresh or dried herbs for garnish—cilantro, parsley, basil, or thyme are good choices.

Preparation
1. Preheat oven to 350° F.
2. Slice squash lengthwise in half. Remove seeds with spoon and discard.
3. Place squash halves, cut-side down, on coconut oil-greased baking sheet and place in oven for 45 minutes. Check at 10-minute intervals after 35 minutes of baking to determine if flesh is fork-tender. Once flesh is fork-tender, remove squash from oven and cool on rack until you can handle it comfortably.
4. Using spoon, scoop flesh from skin and into food processor. Add ¾ of coconut milk and process until smooth (If you don't have a food processor, use a hand mixer or potato masher in a large bowl).
5. Add more coconut milk, as needed, to thin the soup. Place in saucepan and season with salt and pepper, as desired.
6. Ladle soup into bowls and garnish with herbs. For a more dramatic presentation, pour tablespoon of coconut milk over top of soup to create a swirl in soup using spoon. Garnish with fresh or dried herbs before serving. Serve warm or at room temperature.

Goulash

SERVES 2–3

Ingredients

2 Tbsp cooking fat (lard or tallow are good choices)

½ lb beef sirloin or stewing beef, cut in cubes

2 medium onions, sliced

1 bell pepper, sliced

1 garlic clove, minced

2 Tbsp paprika, more if desired

2 tsp caraway seeds

15 oz diced tomatoes, canned or 3 fresh tomatoes, chopped

1½ cups of beef stock (page 243)

Fresh parsley, chopped, for garnish (optional)

Preparation

1. Preheat oven to 350° F, or use slow cooker if you prefer to set it and forget it!
2. Place Dutch oven over medium-high heat with 1 Tbsp of cooking fat. When fat is melted, add beef cubes to Dutch oven and cook until browned on all sides.
3. Remove beef from Dutch oven and set aside. Add onions and remaining cooking fat and sauté for 3 minutes. Add bell pepper and sauté for 5 minutes. Add garlic and sauté for 30 seconds.
4. Place beef back in Dutch oven along with remaining ingredients (except parsley for garnish) and mix well with wooden spoon.
5. Cover Dutch oven and place in preheated oven. Bake preparation for 2 hours, or until beef is fork-tender.

Slow cooker: Follow directions exactly, but do not place in oven. Instead, place all ingredients in the slow cooker and cook for 4–6 hours on low, or until beef is fork-tender.

{ Salads }

Zesty Scallop Salad

SERVES 4

Ingredients

Dressing

3 Tbsp lemon juice

⅛ tsp cayenne pepper, ground

1 Tbsp Paleo Mayonnaise (page 211)

1 tsp Paleo Mustard (page 216)

½ cup olive oil

Salad

1 bell pepper (any color), seeded and cut into strips

1 avocado, peeled, pitted, and cubed

1 garlic clove, minced

2 tsp freshly ground black pepper

½ tsp cayenne pepper, ground

1 tsp sea salt

2 Tbsp coconut oil, for cooking scallops

1 lb small sea or bay scallops (thawed if frozen)

4 cups mixed salad greens

Preparation

Dressing

1. Add lemon juice, cayenne pepper, mayonnaise, and mustard to bowl; whisk until well combined. Slowly drizzle olive oil into mixture, whisking constantly to emulsify. Set aside.

Salad

1. Chop and prepare all vegetables and set aside. Arrange salad greens on plates or in bowls. Sprinkle with chopped vegetables.

2. Place scallops in colander and rinse with cool water. Drain and gently pat dry with paper towels. Place scallops in bowl and sprinkle with garlic, cayenne, salt, and pepper. Toss to coat.

3. Add coconut oil to non-stick skillet over medium heat. Once melted and the skillet is hot, add scallops and sear for 1 minute per side, or until opaque and slightly firm. Remove scallops from skillet immediately (Overcooked scallops are rubbery and unappetizing).

4. Arrange scallops over the vegetables and salad greens. Drizzle with vinaigrette. Serve immediately.

Chicken and Zucchini Salad

SERVES 4

Ingredients

---

3 Tbsp coconut oil

2½ lbs chicken breasts, boneless and skinless, cut into 1-inch cubes

1 large onion, chopped

5 medium zucchini, cut into 1-inch cubes

1 Tbsp dried oregano

7 Tbsp Paleo Mayonnaise (page 211)

Juice of 2 lemons or 3 limes

2 garlic cloves, minced

4 cups chopped Romaine lettuce or baby spinach

Sea salt and freshly ground pepper, to taste

¼ cup raw sliced almonds, for topping

Preparation

1. Heat non-stick skillet over medium-high heat with 1 Tbsp coconut oil, and cook chicken cubes until cooked through and firm, about 6–8 minutes. Remove chicken from skillet and keep warm.
2. To same skillet, add 1 Tbsp coconut oil to melt. Add onion and cook until translucent, 5–7 minutes. Remove onions to small bowl.
3. Add remaining coconut oil and zucchini cubes to skillet. Sprinkle with oregano, salt, and pepper, and cook until zucchini cubes are crisp-tender, about 2–3 minutes.
4. In medium bowl, mix mayonnaise, lemon or lime juice, and minced garlic.
5. Add hot cooked chicken, onion, and zucchini to mayonnaise preparation and mix well. Place chicken salad in refrigerator to cool.
6. When ready to serve, add romaine lettuce to chicken salad, mix well, and serve in bowls. Garnish with almonds, if desired.

Salmon Salad

SERVES 3

Ingredients

3 wild-caught salmon fillets, ½ inch thick
1½ Tbsp coconut oil, for cooking salmon
5–6 Tbsp olive oil
Juice of 2 lemons
2 medium cucumbers, diced
1 medium onion, diced
3 Roma tomatoes, diced
1 medium avocado, peeled, pitted, and diced
2 Tbsp fresh dill, chopped (optional)
Sea salt and ground black pepper, to taste
Lettuce leaves for serving

Preparation

1. Heat coconut oil in non-stick skillet over medium-high heat. Once skillet is hot, add salmon and pan-sear on each side for about 1 minute. Remove from heat, cover, and let sit for 2–3 minutes. It will continue cooking without drying out. Remove salmon to plate or bowl, and cover with plastic wrap. Place in refrigerator to cool.
2. Use fork to shred cooled salmon in bowl.
3. Add lemon juice, olive oil, sea salt, and ground black pepper to salmon, and gently mix to combine. Add cucumbers, onion, tomato, and avocado. Gently fold into the mixture.
4. Arrange lettuce leaves on plate and top with salmon salad. Sprinkle with fresh or dried dill, and serve.

Broccoli Salad

Ingredients

12 to 16 oz broccoli florets

1½ cups red or green grapes, halved

½ medium onion, chopped

½ cup almonds, slivered

1¼ cup Paleo Mayonnaise (page 211) or coconut milk

¼ cup lemon or lime juice

Preparation
1. Mix broccoli florets with almonds, chopped onion, and halved grapes.
2. In separate bowl, mix mayonnaise or coconut milk with lemon or lime juice.
3. Add dressing to salad, mix well, and serve.

Waldorf Chicken Salad

SERVES 4

Ingredients

8 Tbsp Paleo Mayonnaise (page 211) or coconut milk
2 Tbsp lemon or lime juice
Sea salt and freshly ground black pepper, to taste
1 cup walnuts, chopped
1 cup celery, diced
2 red apples, cored and sliced
¼ cup green onions, sliced
1 cup fresh grapes
1 cup chicken, cooked and cubed
Lettuce leaves

Preparation

1. Mix mayonnaise or coconut milk and lemon or lime juice in bowl, and season with salt and pepper to taste. Add walnuts, celery, apples, green onions, grapes, and chicken. Mix well to combine. Serve salad on bed of lettuce leaves.

{ Stir-Frys }

Egg Stir-Fry

Ingredients

1 Tbsp coconut oil or tallow

6 large eggs

4 Roma tomatoes, sliced into wedges

2 green onions, thinly sliced

Sea salt and ground black pepper, to taste

Preparation

1. Whisk eggs in bowl. Heat wok or non-stick skillet with half the cooking fat. Once fat has melted, add eggs and stir-fry for one minute. Remove eggs and set aside.

2. Add remaining cooking fat to wok. Add tomatoes and stir-fry for 2 minutes. Return eggs to skillet along with green onions and stir-fry 30 more seconds. Sprinkle with salt and pepper to taste. Serve immediately.

Curry Chicken Stir-Fry

Ingredients

1 tsp curry powder

1 tsp ginger root, grated

15 oz coconut milk

1 Tbsp coconut oil

1 lb skinless chicken breasts, cut into thin slices

¼ cup onion, chopped

2 cups broccoli florets, cut into bite-sized pieces

3 cups spinach, packed

3 Tbsp coconut, grated (or unsweetened coconut flakes)

Preparation

1. Add coconut milk, curry powder, and grated ginger to bowl, and whisk to combine. Set aside.
2. Add coconut oil to wok over high heat. Once wok is hot, add chicken and stir-fry until cooked through, 5–6 minutes. Remove chicken from wok and set aside.
3. Add more coconut oil to wok, then the onion, and stir-fry for 2 minutes. Add broccoli florets and stir-fry an additional 3 minutes.
4. Return chicken to wok along with curry sauce and spinach. As soon as spinach wilts, remove chicken mixture and plate it. Spoon leftover sauce over top and sprinkle with grated (or flaked) coconut. Serve warm.

Beef Heart Stir-Fry

SERVES 2

Ingredients

1 Tbsp coconut oil or tallow

1 lb beef heart

1½ cups zucchini, cubed

1 tsp fresh ginger root, grated

Juice of 1 lime or lemon

1 chili pepper, thinly sliced for cooking

Preparation

1. Remove fat and connective tissue from beef heart, and cut heart into bite-sized cubes.

2. Heat wok over medium-high heat with oil. Add heart cubes and stir-fry 3–5 minutes, or to desired doneness. Remove heart cubes from wok and set aside.

3. Add more cooking fat to wok and stir-fry zucchini for 1 minute. Add grated ginger root, lime or lemon juice, and most of the hot pepper slices (reserve some for garnish), and stir-fry for 1 minute. Return heart cubes to wok and stir-fry for 1 more minute.

4. Serve warm, garnished with sliced hot peppers.

Basil Pesto Chicken Stir-Fry

SERVES 2–3

Ingredients

2 cups basil leaves

¼ cup pine nuts, toasted

¼ cup olive oil

1 Tbsp coconut oil

1 lb boneless and skinless chicken breasts, cut in thin strips

1 medium onion, sliced

1 lb mushrooms of any kind, in small chunks

Preparation

1. Process basil leaves and toasted pine nuts in food processor, and slowly add olive oil until smooth consistency is reached.
2. Heat wok over medium-high heat with about half the coconut oil. Add chicken pieces and stir-fry until cooked through, 4–5 minutes. Remove chicken from wok and set aside.
3. Add any remaining coconut oil to wok and stir-fry onion for 3–4 minutes. Add mushrooms and stir-fry for another 2 minutes.
4. Return chicken to wok, add basil pesto, and stir well. Cook for another 2–3 minutes until everything is heated through. Serve immediately.

Poultry and Oranges Stir-Fry

SERVES 2–3

Ingredients

1 Tbsp coconut oil

4 lbs roasted duck or rotisserie-roasted chicken

1 medium onion, sliced

2 tsp fresh ginger root, grated

2 garlic cloves, minced

1 Tbsp orange zest

⅔ cup orange juice

¼ cup chicken stock (page 243)

2 lbs bok choy, baby spinach, or mixed baby greens

1 medium orange, peeled and segmented (or more if desired)

Preparation

1. Pick meat from roasted duck or chicken and set aside.
2. Heat wok over medium-high heat with coconut oil. Add onion, and stir-fry it for 2 minutes. Add grated ginger and stir-fry for 1 minute. Add garlic and stir-fry 30 more seconds.
3. Add orange juice, orange zest, and chicken stock, and bring to a boil. Add meat to the wok, reduce heat, and let simmer for 2 minutes.
4. Remove meat from wok, add bok choy (or greens of choice), and cook until just wilted.
5. Serve meat on bed of wilted greens, topped with the sauce left in wok and garnished with orange segments.

Ginger Pork Stir-Fry

Ingredients

1 Tbsp ginger root, minced
4 garlic cloves, minced
1 cup cilantro leaves
¼ cup olive oil
1 lb pork tenderloin, thinly sliced
1 Tbsp coconut oil
1 bell pepper, thinly sliced
1 Tbsp lime or lemon juice
2 medium onions, thinly sliced

Preparation

1. Add minced ginger, garlic, half of the cilantro and all of the olive oil to bowl and mix well. Place pork in bowl with olive oil mixture, and stir to coat the pork thoroughly. Place pork, covered, in refrigerator to marinate for 1–4 hours.
2. Once pork has marinated thoroughly, heat wok over medium-high heat with coconut oil. When the wok is hot, add pork slices and stir-fry 3–4 minutes, or until cooked through. Remove pork from wok and keep warm.
3. Add a little more coconut oil to wok, add onions, and stir-fry for 2 minutes. Add bell pepper and stir-fry for 3 minutes more.
4. Return pork to wok along with lime or lemon juice and remaining cilantro leaves. Stir-fry for 1 minute. Toss to combine well, and serve hot.

Minted Beef Stir-Fry

SERVES 2–3

Ingredients

1 lb beef tenderloin, cut into thin slices

3 red chilies, finely chopped

3 garlic cloves, minced

1 Tbsp coconut oil

12 asparagus spears, chopped

2 Tbsp beef stock or water (page 243)

1 cup fresh mint leaves

Thinly sliced red chili for garnishing

Preparation

1. Mix beef, chopped chilies, garlic, and stock or water in bowl. Cover and refrigerate for at least 2 hours to marinate.
2. Heat wok over medium-high heat with coconut oil. Add beef strips and stir-fry for 3–4 minutes or until cooked through. Remove beef and keep warm.
3. Add a little more coconut oil to wok. Once melted, add chopped asparagus, and stir-fry 1–2 minutes. Add ¼ cup stock or water if necessary.
4. Return cooked beef strips along with mint to wok and cook for 1 minute. Plate beef with juices, and garnish with sliced red chili pepper.

Citrus and Spinach Beef Stir-Fry

SERVES 2–3

Ingredients

1 lemon, peeled and segmented
1 orange, peeled and segmented
2 Tbsp coconut oil or tallow
1 lb beef sirloin, cut into thin strips
1 medium onion, sliced
2 garlic cloves, minced
1 tsp ginger, minced or grated
1 tsp lemon or lime zest
1 tsp orange zest
1 Tbsp lemon or lime juice
1 Tbsp orange juice
2 cups baby spinach, tightly packed

Preparation

1. Arrange segmented lemons and oranges on server plate.
2. Heat wok over medium-high heat with 1 Tbsp coconut fat or tallow. Once wok is hot, add beef and stir-fry for 3–4 minutes, or until cooked through. Remove beef from wok and keep warm.
3. Add remaining coconut oil or tallow to wok. Place onion, garlic, ginger, and lemon or lime zest in wok and stir-fry for 3–5 minutes or until onions are translucent.
4. Return beef to wok along with lemon or lime juice and orange juice. Bring liquid to a boil and add spinach to wok, tossing to coat. Cook until spinach is just wilted. Remove all ingredients from wok and plate on top of segmented lemons and oranges. Serve immediately.

Citrus Shrimp Stir-Fry

Ingredients

1 onion, very finely chopped

¼ cup olive oil

1 Tbsp lemon or lime zest

3 garlic cloves, minced

½ cup lemon or lime juice

2 small red chilies, seeded and finely chopped

2 Tbsp coconut oil

1 Tbsp ginger root, grated

1 tsp turmeric

20–24 raw shrimp, shelled, deveined, and rinsed

Preparation

1. Add onion, olive oil, lemon or lime juice and zest, garlic, chilies, ginger, and turmeric to bowl and whisk. Place shrimp in bowl with marinade, cover and refrigerate for 8 hours.
2. After shrimp have marinated, remove from marinade with slotted spoon, and reserve marinade.
3. Heat wok over medium-high heat with coconut oil. When wok is hot, add shrimp and stir-fry until pink, only about 2 minutes. Do not overcook. Turn shrimp over at least once. Remove from wok and keep warm.
4. Add reserved marinade to wok and bring to a boil, stirring constantly. Boil marinade for about 2 minutes, then plate shrimp, and pour marinade over top.

{ Poultry }

Curry Chicken

Ingredients

3 Tbsp coconut oil

1 medium onion, diced

2 lbs skinless, boneless chicken thighs, chopped

1 cup coconut milk

¼ cup lemon or lime juice

½ cup chicken stock (page 243)

3–4 garlic cloves, minced

1 Tbsp ground coriander or ¼ cup fresh cilantro leaves, chopped

⅓ cup dried mint or 1 cup fresh mint leaves, chopped

1 medium hot pepper, diced

1¼ tsp turmeric

½ tsp cinnamon

½ tsp ground cardamom

⅛ tsp ground cloves

Sea salt and freshly ground black pepper, to taste

Preparation

1. Heat non-stick skillet over medium heat and add coconut oil. Once oil is melted, add onion and sauté until translucent, 5–7 minutes. Add chicken to skillet and cook until firm, stirring occasionally—about 5 minutes.

2. While chicken is cooking, add lemon or lime juice, chicken stock, coriander or cilantro, mint, hot pepper, and garlic to blender or food processor and process until mixture is smooth.

3. To skillet, add turmeric, cinnamon, cardamom, and cloves. Stir to coat chicken with spices. Add coconut milk to skillet and season to taste with salt and pepper. Next, add herb purée and stir. Bring to a simmer and cook for 30–45 minutes, until flavors bloom.

Your choice of hot pepper depends on your desired level of spiciness. Serrano, jalapeño, and poblano are good choices. Serrano is the hottest, followed by the jalapeño, and the mildest is the poblano.

Spicy Chicken with Spinach Herb Sauce

Ingredients for chicken

1 Tbsp ground chipotle

1 Tbsp smoked paprika

2 tsp ground cumin

2 tsp dry mustard

2 tsp ground thyme

1 tsp freshly ground black pepper

2 tsp sea salt

4 medium chicken breasts, boneless and
skinless

2–4 Tbsp coconut oil or tallow for frying

Ingredients for herb sauce

½ cup olive oil

2 cups fresh mint leaves

1 cup baby spinach

5 garlic cloves, minced

2 Tbsp Dijon Style Mustard (page 219)

1 jalapeño pepper, seeded and chopped
(optional)

Sea salt and freshly ground black pepper,
to taste

Preparation

Spinach Herb Sauce

1. Place mint, spinach, garlic, jalapeño pepper, Dijon mustard, salt and ground black pepper in a food processor and process with a rough chop. Slowly drizzle olive oil in the processor to create a stable emulsion. A stable emulsion is formed when all ingredients are in solution and do not separate after standing at room temperature for 5–10 minutes.

Chicken

1. Combine the ground chipotle, paprika, cumin, dry mustard, thyme, salt and pepper in a bowl. Rub the chicken breasts all over with your chosen cooking fat and sprinkle both sides with the spice rub mixture. Heat a non-stick skillet over medium-high heat, place remaining cooking fat in the skillet, and fry chicken breasts for 3–5 minutes per side, or until internal temperature reads 160°–165° F with a meat thermometer.

2. Serve the spicy chicken warm, topped with the fresh herb sauce.

Fajitas

Ingredients

3 lbs boneless and skinless chicken breasts, cut in thin strips or top sirloin steak, sliced thinly

3 bell peppers (multi-colored), sliced thinly

2 jalapeño peppers, seeded and sliced (optional)

3 medium onions, sliced

½ Tbsp dried oregano

½ Tbsp chili powder

½ Tbsp ground cumin

½ Tbsp ground coriander

6 garlic cloves, minced

Juice of 5 lemons or 6 limes

4 Tbsp cooking fat (coconut oil or tallow)

Lettuce leaves to use as wrap

Preparation

1. Combine all ingredients except cooking fat, mix well, and cover. Place in refrigerator for 1–4 hours to marinate.

2. When ready to cook, heat cooking fat in large non-stick skillet over medium heat. Cook entire preparation in cooking fat until chicken or steak is cooked through, peppers are crisp-tender, and onions are translucent, 5–7 minutes.

3. While fajita filling is cooking, prepare lettuce leaves on platter and place on table or buffet line. When meat mixture is done, place hot fajita preparation in large bowl or on serving platter set on table or buffet, with lettuce and other fajita toppings. Ask your guests or family to prepare their own fajitas wrapped in lettuce leaves and covered with their favorite toppings.

Arrange a table or buffet line with your favorite fajita ingredients, such as diced tomatoes, sliced jalapeño peppers, sliced avocados, salsa, guacamole, and salsa verde (page 239).

Garlic Lime Chicken

SERVES 4

Ingredients

¼ cup coconut oil

8 chicken thighs, with bones and skin

½ lb Kalamata olives, halved

3 cups onion, thinly sliced

30 garlic cloves, minced and smashed

1½ cups chicken stock (page 243)

½ cup lime or lemon juice

2 extra limes or lemons, thickly sliced, with seeds removed

One bunch of picked thyme leaves or 1 teaspoon of dried thyme

Sea salt and freshly ground black pepper, to taste

Preparation

1. Preheat oven to 350° F.
2. Melt ⅔ of coconut oil in large oven-safe pan or Dutch oven over medium-high heat. Brown chicken pieces on all sides, cooking for about 6 minutes total. Set chicken aside.
3. Add remaining cooking fat to skillet and sauté onions until translucent, 5–7 minutes, scraping sides and bottom of pan to capture crispy bits.
4. Add garlic and cook for about 30 seconds, until fragrant. Add chicken stock, lemon or lime juice, and season with salt and pepper. Return chicken to pan, skin-side up. Bring to a simmer and transfer pan, covered, to oven for 20 minutes.
5. Remove lid, add halved olives and lemon slices, and bake for another 15 minutes, uncovered. Serve chicken with olive, garlic, and lemon sauce. Garnish with lemon or lime slices.

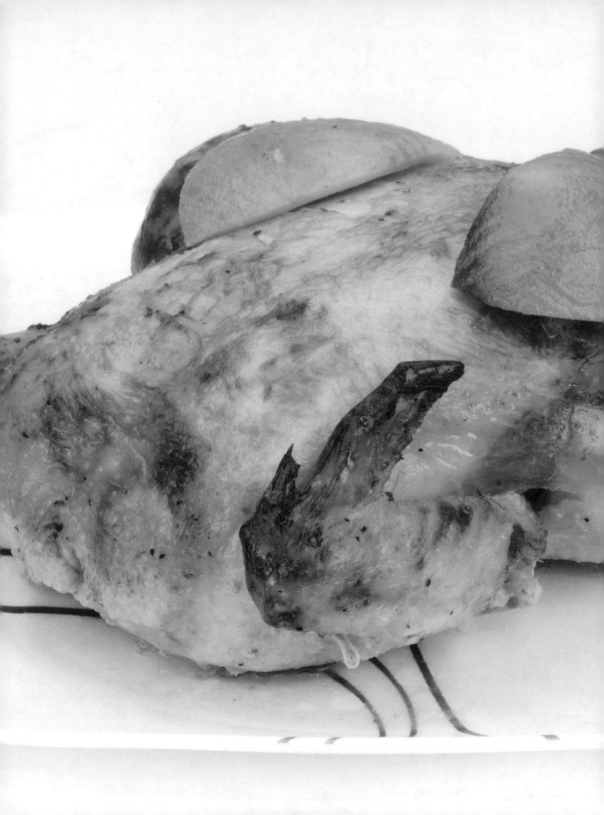

Ginger Lime Chicken

SERVES 4

Ingredients

5 Tbsp cooking fat (coconut oil, lard, or tallow), melted

3 medium limes or lemons

2 medium oranges

1 whole chicken, about 4 lbs

3 Tbsp ginger root, grated

Sea salt and freshly ground black pepper, to taste

2 extra oranges and 2 extra lemons or limes to be used as garnish

Preparation

1. Preheat oven to 425° F.
2. Grate zest of one orange and one lime or lemon, and then cut each one into quarters. Set aside.
3. Wipe chicken dry and place it in roasting pan.
4. Mix 1 Tbsp of grated ginger with citrus zest. Rub citrus-ginger mixture in chicken cavity with some added salt and pepper. Place quartered lemon or lime and orange inside cavity of chicken.
5. Juice remaining limes/lemons and orange. Mix juice with remaining 2 Tbsp grated ginger root and melted coconut oil. Brush outside of chicken with this mixture.
6. Place chicken in oven and roast for 15 minutes. Baste with juice mixture, and reduce heat to 375° F. Place chicken back in oven and roast for 25 minutes. Baste again and return to oven for another 25 minutes.
7. Remove chicken from oven and test for doneness, using meat thermometer inserted in thickest part of breast and in thigh. Temperature should be at least 160° F in breast and at least 170° F in thigh.
8. When chicken is done, remove it from oven, and allow it to sit for 15 minutes. Garnish with extra citrus wedges, and plate on platter surrounded by steamed vegetables or greens, if desired. Use any cooking juices gathered in roasting pan as sauce to be served with chicken.

"Butter" Chicken

Ingredients

4 Tbsp coconut oil, divided

2 lbs chicken, cut in chunks

2 tsp garam masala (more or less to taste)

2 tsp paprika

2 tsp ground coriander

1 Tbsp fresh ginger root, grated

¼ tsp ground red pepper (adjust to taste)

1 cinnamon stick

6 cardamom pods, bruised

15 oz pureed canned tomatoes or fresh, ripe, meaty tomatoes
   (Roma tomatoes work nicely)

¾ cup coconut milk

1 Tbsp fresh lemon juice

Fresh herbs and cinnamon sticks for garnish (optional)

Preparation

1. Heat non-stick skillet or wok over medium-high heat with half of the coconut oil. When oil is melted, add chicken and stir-fry until cooked through. Remove cooked chicken from the skillet and set aside. Reduce the heat to low.

2. Add remaining coconut oil to skillet. When oil is melted, add spices and mix well to combine. Place skillet or wok over low heat and simmer for 1–2 minutes, or just until you begin to smell spice aroma. Immediately add cooked chicken and tomatoes to skillet or wok and stir. Simmer chicken mixture for 15 minutes, stirring occasionally.

3. Add coconut milk to chicken mixture, stir, and simmer for 5 minutes, stirring occasionally.

4. Using large serving spoon, plate chicken with coconut sauce, and garnish with fresh herbs and a cinnamon stick, if desired.

Turkey Burgers

Ingredients

1 Tbsp coconut oil

1 lb turkey, ground

1 cup cilantro, chopped

¼ cup red onion, diced

2 garlic cloves, minced

¾ tsp sea salt

¼ tsp freshly ground black pepper

Olive oil for basting

Preparation

1. Heat stovetop griddle or outdoor grill to medium-high heat.
2. Combine all ingredients, except coconut and olive oil, in bowl and mix well. Divide meat preparation into 4 portions, and shape into ½-inch thick patties.
3. Brush grill with coconut oil. Grill until cooked to desired doneness as determined with meat thermometer inserted in center of patty. Medium doneness is 140°–150° F on grill. Baste with olive oil as needed. Meat will continue to cook after you remove from cooking surface. Serve warm.

{ Pork }

Pork Tenderloin with Fruit and Onions

Ingredients

---

2 Tbsp cooking fat + extra for rubbing on the pork, melted (see page xii)

30–36 oz pork tenderloin, trimmed of fat and silver skin, sliced in 1-inch thick portions

3 nectarines or 4 apricots, seeded and quartered

1 large onion, quartered

2 tsp Dijon Style Mustard (page 219)

1½ Tbsp lime or lemon juice

¼ cup fresh basil, coarsely chopped

Sea salt and freshly ground black pepper, to taste

Preparation

1. Heat non-stick skillet over medium-high heat and melt cooking fat – coconut oil or animal tallow.

2. Add nectarine and onion quarters to skillet and season with salt and pepper to taste. Remove fruit and onion from skillet to bowl once heated through, about 2–3 minutes. Pour any remaining juices from skillet over fruit and onions. Keep warm. Wipe skillet with paper towel.

3. Rub cooking fat over pork slices on both sides and season them to taste with salt and pepper. Reheat skillet over medium-high heat until hot. Add pork to hot skillet and sear for 3 minutes per side.

4. While tenderloins are searing, cut cooked fruit and onion quarters into slices. Place them back in bowl and add lime or lemon juice, mustard, and chopped basil. Adjust seasoning with salt and pepper as desired.

5. Plate pork and top with fruit and onion preparation, pouring accumulated juices over top. Garnish with fresh basil leaves.

Zingy Pulled Pork

SERVES 8–10

Pulled pork ingredients

1 pork shoulder or butt roast, about 5 lbs

3 Tbsp ground chipotle (more or less to taste)

1 Tbsp garlic powder

1 Tbsp dry mustard

3 Tbsp sea salt

Zingy barbecue sauce

1 cup apple cider vinegar

1 cup Paleo Ketchup (page 212)

1 cup Paleo Mustard (page 216)

2 Tbsp of honey (to taste)

2 garlic cloves, minced

1 tsp cayenne pepper, ground

1 tsp sea salt

½ tsp freshly ground black pepper

Preparation

1. Rub: Combine chipotle, garlic powder, dry mustard, and sea salt in bowl. Whisk with fork.
2. Rub pork butt all over with spice rub and refrigerate in covered container for 1–2 hours.
3. Fifteen minutes before pork butt is ready to bake, preheat oven to 300° F.
4. Place pork butt in oven in baking pan deep enough to catch all juices that will seep from pork. Bake for 5–6 hours, or until meat is falling apart and extremely tender. Do not over-bake and dry out.
5. While pork is baking, prepare barbecue sauce by combining vinegar, ketchup, mustard, honey, garlic, cayenne pepper, salt, and pepper in small saucepan. Bring to a simmer and cook, stirring occasionally, for 7–10 minutes, until flavors are fully combined and sauce has thickened slightly. Adjust seasonings to taste.
6. Remove pork from oven and rest for a minimum of 10 minutes, (preferably 20–30 minutes), to allow juices to redistribute.
7. Separate or "pull" meat apart using two forks. Place pulled pork in large serving bowl and toss with barbecue sauce or serve sauce on the side. Serve warm.

Pork Tenderloin with Apples and Onions

SERVES 4

Ingredients

24–32 oz pork tenderloin, fat and silver skin removed, in 1-inch slices

3 Tbsp coconut oil or lard

2 large onions, sliced

4 apples, cored and sliced

Sea salt and ground black pepper, to taste

Preparation

1. Heat large non-stick skillet over medium-high heat with 2 Tbsp cooking fat. Season pork tenderloins with salt and pepper to taste.
2. Add tenderloins to skillet and sear (uncovered) for about 5 minutes on each side, or until internal temperature reaches at least 145° F as measured with meat thermometer.
3. Remove pork from skillet and set aside. Reduce heat to medium-low, then add remaining cooking fat, onions, and apples.
4. Cook for about 10–15 minutes, until onions have browned and apple slices are softened.
5. Serve tenderloin slices topped with apples and onions.

Sausage Pizza

Ingredients

2 tsp olive oil

1 cup almond flour

3 Tbsp nut butter
(cashew or almond)

⅓ cup egg whites

2 tsp coconut oil

½ cup onion, diced

2 garlic cloves, minced

1 hot pepper, chopped
(more or less as desired)

¾ cup cherry tomatoes,
halved

8 oz sausage, sliced or crum-
bled (low sodium and no
artificial ingredients)

½ cup marinara sauce or
crushed tomatoes

½ tsp oregano

½ tsp caraway seeds

Preparation

1. Preheat oven to 250° F.
2. Add almond flour, nut butter, and egg whites to bowl. Mix with hands to combine well and create pizza dough. Set aside.
3. In non-stick skillet over medium-high heat, brown sausage until completely cooked through. Remove sausage from skillet and place in small bowl.
4. Add onions, hot pepper, and a little coconut oil to same skillet and sauté until onions are translucent, 5–7 minutes. Add garlic to onion preparation and sauté for 30 seconds. Remove onion mixture from skillet and set aside.
5. Cover baking pan with olive oil. Roll dough mixture with rolling pin to ¼-inch thickness on flat surface, and then press evenly into oiled pizza pan.
6. Spread marinara sauce evenly across dough. Arrange meat and onion mixture evenly atop marinara sauce. Sprinkle toppings with oregano and caraway seeds. Use more seasonings if pizza sauce is plain crushed tomatoes instead marinara sauce.
7. Place pizza in oven and bake for 30 minutes or until pizza dough is slightly crisp. Remove pizza from oven and add halved tomatoes. Slice pizza into eight pieces and serve warm.

Chef's Notes: This is a basic pizza recipe. Feel free to alter the recipe to include your favorite paleo herbs, spices, vegetables, meats, and sauces.

{ Beef and Bison }

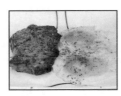

Steak and Eggs

SERVES 1

Ingredients

8 oz beef steak (filet, sirloin, or ribeye), 1 inch thick

3 Tbsp coconut oil or tallow

2 large eggs

Paprika, to taste

Sea salt and pepper, to taste

Preparation

1. Heat non-stick pan over medium-high heat and add 2 Tbsp of your chosen cooking fat.
2. Season both sides of steak with salt and pepper, and place it in hot pan. Cook steak to desired doneness, about 2–3 minutes on each side for medium rare, or about 4–5 minutes per side for medium doneness. You can also use meat thermometer inserted in center to determine doneness. Keep in mind that steak will continue to cook for 1–2 minutes after being removed from pan. Remove steak from pan, and let it rest to allow juices to redistribute.
3. Reduce temperature to medium-low, and add rest of cooking fat to same skillet.
4. Crack eggs into hot pan, season to taste with some paprika, salt and pepper, then cover and cook until whites are just set.
5. Serve steak warm, with eggs on top.

Liver and Onions

SERVES 5

Ingredients

4 large slices beef, pork, or lamb liver

5 medium onions, sliced

6 Tbsp coconut oil, tallow, or lard

Sea salt and black pepper, to taste

Preparation

1. Heat large non-stick skillet over medium-low heat and add 5 Tbsp cooking fat and sliced onions. Cook slowly, stirring often, for about 20 to 25 minutes, until onions are soft and caramelized.

2. When onions are nearly done, heat another non-stick skillet over medium-high heat and add remaining cooking fat. Once fat is melted, add liver slices, and sear for 3 minutes on each side.

3. Serve liver warm, topped with caramelized onions.

Oxtail Vihannes

SERVES 4

Ingredients

2 oxtails, each cut into 4 sections

½ cup carrots, chopped

½ cup onions, diced

½ cup celery, chopped

½ cup leeks, chopped

4 Tbsp cooking fat (coconut oil, tallow or lard)

1 lb Roma tomatoes, whole

8 sprigs fresh thyme

2 bay leaves

4 garlic cloves, minced

4½ cups beef or chicken stock (page 243)

Vihannes

1 carrot, diced

1 onion, diced

2 celery stalks, diced

½ medium leek, diced

4 Roma tomatoes, diced

2 Tbsp fresh parsley, chopped

Preparation

1. Preheat oven to 350° F. Heat cooking fat in Dutch oven. When Dutch oven is hot, add oxtail, and brown on each side. Remove and set aside.
2. Add vegetables to Dutch oven and brown them in remaining cooking fat. Scrape off any meat or vegetable residue from the bottom of pan with wooden spoon. Once vegetables are browned, add whole tomatoes, thyme sprigs, bay leaves, and minced garlic. Cook for 2 minutes, stirring constantly.
3. Place oxtail back in Dutch oven and add enough stock to completely cover the pieces.
4. Bring stock to a simmer and cover. Place Dutch oven in preheated oven and bake for 2 hours.
5. Remove from oven and discard bay leaves.

Vihannes

1. Bring pot of water to a boil. Place fresh vegetables in boiling water and blanch for 3 minutes. Strain pot of water and vegetables through colander. Add blanched vegetables to oxtail and simmer for 2 more minutes on stovetop. Plate mixture and enjoy immediately.

Bison Chili

Ingredients

1 Tbsp coconut oil

1¾ lbs ground bison

½ medium onion, chopped

2½ cups celery, chopped

2 garlic cloves

12 oz salsa, bottled

8 oz diced tomatoes, canned

2 tsp cumin

2 tsp chili powder

2 tsp thyme leaves, fresh

2 tsp sea salt

¼ cup mild green chilies, diced

Tomato juice for thinning (if desired)

Preparation

1. Heat coconut oil in Dutch oven over medium-high heat. When oil is melted, add onions and celery, and sauté until onions are translucent, about 5–7 minutes. Add garlic and sauté for 30 more seconds. Immediately add ground meat, cumin, thyme, and chili powder. Stir.

2. Cook for 5 minutes, or until meat is thoroughly browned, stirring often. Add salsa, tomatoes, mild green chilies and sea salt to Dutch oven and stir. Reduce heat and simmer for one hour, covered, stirring often. Thin with tomato juice or water if desired. Serve warm.

Chef's note: Bison is lean and tasty. However, you may use any lean ground meat. Beef venison, and elk are all good choices.

Traditional Meatloaf

SERVES 3–4

Ingredients

---

1 Tbsp coconut oil or tallow

1½ lbs lean ground beef, bison, or elk

1 cup almond milk

¼ tsp dried sage

½ tsp salt

½ tsp dry mustard

¼ tsp fresh ground pepper

2 garlic cloves, minced

1 small onion, finely chopped

½ cup cabbage, chopped

1 cup Paleo Barbecue Sauce (page 233)

Preparation

1. Preheat oven to 350° F.
2. Combine all ingredients except barbecue sauce in large bowl, and mix well to combine.
3. Place mixture into ungreased loaf pan or shape into loaf on ungreased rimmed baking sheet.
4. Bake, uncovered, for about one hour. When internal temperature reaches 140°F (measure thickest part of loaf), pour barbecue sauce over top of meatloaf and return it to oven for another 15–20 minutes of bake time. Sauce will caramelize a little, and meatloaf will finish cooking through.
5. Remove meatloaf from oven and let it rest for 10 minutes to allow juices to redistribute. Slice and serve warm.

"Spaghetti" with Meat Sauce

SERVES 2

Ingredients

One medium spaghetti
   squash
½ lb ground bison or beef
1 Tbsp cooking fat (coconut
   oil or tallow)
½ large onion, diced
2 garlic cloves, minced
1½ carrots, diced

1 celery stick, diced
1 tsp dried basil
1 tsp dried oregano
1 Tbsp tomato paste
1 bay leaf
35 oz whole canned
   tomatoes, cut up

2–4 Tbsp coconut milk
   (optional)
¼ tsp red pepper flakes
   (optional)
Sea salt and freshly ground
   black pepper, to taste
Fresh parsley, oregano, or
   basil for garnish

Preparation

1. Heat cooking fat in large Dutch oven over medium-high heat. Add ground bison or beef, and brown for 5 minutes or until cooked through. If your ground meat has higher fat content, use less or even no cooking fat. Remove cooked ground meat with slotted spoon and set aside.

2. Add carrots, celery, onion, garlic, basil, and oregano to Dutch oven and cook until softened, about 5–7 minutes. Then add cut-up tomatoes and their juice, tomato paste, cooked ground meat, and bay leaf. Season with red pepper flakes, salt and pepper to taste. Bring mixture to a boil and then reduce heat to a simmer for about 40 minutes, stirring occasionally.

3. Fifteen minutes into simmering time, preheat oven to 350° F. Cut spaghetti squash in half lengthwise and remove and discard seeds. Put halves cut-side down on greased baking sheet and place in oven for 25 minutes.

4. Remove from oven. Squash should easily separate into "spaghetti" strands when prodded with ends of fork. Do not overcook or it will turn to mush. Use fork to separate squash into "spaghetti" noodles onto serving plates, and keep them warm.

5. Once your meat sauce is finished simmering, taste it to determine if you'd like to add coconut milk to reduce the tomatoes' acidity. If so, add it now.

6. Spoon meat sauce over plated spaghetti squash and garnish with fresh parsley, oregano, or basil.

{ Fish }

Cooking a Whole Fish

1. When choosing a fish to cook whole, those with a higher fat content work best. Salmon, sea bass, grouper, and trout are good choices. Higher fat content allows for some overcooking without ruining the fish by drying it out.

2. Place in an ovenproof baking dish that fits the fish, so that the cooking fluids stay in contact with the fish while baking. To create complex flavors, place herbs and vegetables under and inside the fish. Consider using lemon slices, fresh dill, garlic cloves, thyme sprigs, sliced onion, rosemary sprigs, carrots, and celery.

3. Because we are talking paleo dining, try doing what our ancestors would have done and some cultures still do today: Eat the entire fish, including the eyes. Save the bones for fumet or fish stock for future soups.

Baked Fish with Asparagus and Roasted Beets

SERVES 4

Ingredients

4 wild salmon fillets (or your favorite wild-caught fish)

4 medium red beets, cut in cubes

16 stalks fresh asparagus (thawed frozen asparagus works, too)

4 Tbsp coconut oil

4 tsp chopped fresh dill or 1½ tsp dried dill

Sea salt and black pepper, to taste

Preparation

1. Preheat oven to 500° F.
2. Tear off four pieces of heavy duty baking foil each large enough to wrap one fish fillet. Make bed of beet cubes in middle of each piece of foil and roast for 15 minutes. Remove beets from oven and allow to cool slightly.
3. Top each bed of beets with 4 stalks of asparagus, and place fillets atop asparagus. Add 1 Tbsp of cooking fat and 1 tsp dill (or sprinkle dried dill evenly) on top of each fillet. Close foil to form packet, seam side up, so juices do not leak.
4. Place foil packs in oven for 10 minutes per inch thickness of fish.
5. Check your fish 7 minutes into cooking to make sure it does not get overcooked and dry. Fish is done when it flakes easily with fork.
6. Open foil packs carefully, so that steam doesn't burn your hand. Remove contents from pack and plate. You can also serve foil pouches directly on each plate. Sprinkle more fresh dill or your favorite herb atop fish. Serve warm.

Lemon Dill Trout

SERVES 2

Ingredients

1 whole trout (or other fish of choice), scaled, gutted, and cleaned
2 Tbsp coconut oil
½ bunch fresh flat leaf parsley, chopped
½ bunch fresh dill, minced
Zest of one lemon
2 lemons, one sliced and the other halved
Salt and freshly ground black pepper, to taste

Preparation

1. Preheat oven broiler.
2. Using knife, slash sides of fish about 6 times on each side to allow coconut oil to get inside.
3. Rub trout with coconut oil and season with salt and pepper.
4. Place chopped parsley, dill, and lemon slices in cavity of trout. Place stuffed trout in snug baking dish. Sprinkle with lemon zest, and place in oven about 6 inches from the coil or flame. Flip trout over after 4–6 minutes of broiling or once golden brown. Broil another 4–6 minutes or until golden brown. Remove from oven.
5. While fish is broiling, juice lemon halves. Pour lemon juice over fish before serving.

Nut-Crusted Salmon

Ingredients

2 Tbsp coconut oil

½ cup nuts, ground into meal (almonds, pecan, or walnuts)

¼ tsp coriander

⅛ tsp cumin

⅛ tsp ground chipotle (optional)

4 salmon fillets or any other paleo fish

2 tsp lemon juice

Sea salt and freshly ground black pepper, to taste

Preparation

1. Preheat oven to 500° F, broiling temperature
2. Combine nut meal (ground, but not buttered) with coriander, cumin, and chipotle (if using) in small bowl, and stir to combine.
3. Coat salmon with lemon juice and season with salt and pepper. Place nut mixture on plate and dredge salmon to coat.
4. Melt coconut oil in non-stick, ovenproof skillet over medium-high heat. Place salmon in skillet skin-side down (if skin remains). Place the skillet in oven, and bake for 10–12 minutes or until flesh flakes easily with fork. Do not over-bake or fish will be dry.

Basil Salmon with Coconut Cream Sauce

Ingredients

1 lb wild salmon, in 1 or 2 fillets

1 tsp coconut oil

2 tsp olive oil

2 Tbsp fresh basil, chopped

3 garlic cloves, minced

1 shallot, diced

Zest of one lemon

Juice of one lemon

½ cup coconut milk

Sea salt and freshly ground black pepper, to taste

Preparation

1. Preheat oven to 350° F.
2. Place salmon on foil-lined rimmed baking sheet greased with coconut oil. Sprinkle fillets with chopped basil, sea salt, and pepper.
3. Heat olive oil in non-stick skillet over medium-high heat, and sauté garlic and shallot for 30 seconds. Immediately add lemon juice, lemon zest, and coconut milk. Stir well. Bring to a gentle boil, then lower the heat to a simmer. Simmer for 2 minutes.
4. Pour coconut milk preparation over salmon. Place salmon in oven and bake for 12–13 minutes, or until salmon flakes easily with fork. Serve warm.

{ Seafood }

Curried Baby Greens and Shrimp

SERVES 4

Ingredients

2 Tbsp coconut oil

1 medium onion, chopped

2 tsp curry powder

2 tsp tomato paste

½ cup chicken stock (page 243)

1 cup coconut milk

2 lbs shrimp, peeled and deveined

4 cups mixed baby greens, chopped

Sea salt and freshly ground black pepper, to taste

Preparation

1. Heat large non-stick skillet over medium-high heat and melt coconut oil. Add onion and sauté until translucent, about 5 or 6 minutes.

2. Season onion with salt and pepper, then stir in curry powder and continue cooking for about 30 seconds.

3. Place skillet mixture, tomato paste, chicken stock, and coconut milk in food processor and process until smooth. Pour mixture back into skillet and use rubber or silicon spatula to scrape sides of processor to add any remaining sauce to skillet.

4. Bring sauce to a simmer. Add shrimp and baby greens. Cover and simmer for 2–3 minutes or until shrimp are pink. Do not overcook.

5. Serve immediately.

Hot Cilantro Shrimp

SERVES 2

Instructions

---

1 lb large or jumbo shrimp, peeled and deveined

1 cup cilantro, rinsed and coarsely chopped

4 jalapeño peppers, seeded and coarsely chopped (for hotter shrimp, do not remove seeds)

4 green onions, thinly sliced

3 cloves garlic, minced

Metal or bamboo skewers (2 for each kebab)

1 tsp freshly ground black pepper

1 tsp ground cumin

½ cup olive oil

¼ cup fresh lime or lemon juice

Preparation

1. Thread shrimp onto 2 parallel skewers, using 2 skewers for each kebab. Arrange kebabs in shallow glass baking dish.

2. Set aside 3 Tbsp of cilantro for garlic cilantro sauce. Place remaining cilantro, jalapeños, green onions, minced garlic, salt, pepper, and cumin in food processor. Turn processor on and gradually add ¼ cup olive oil and ¼ cup lemon or lime juice until smooth marinade solution forms. Remove marinade from food processor and pour over shrimp in glass baking dish. Cover and refrigerate for at least 30 minutes.

3. Heat remaining oil in saucepan over medium heat, add reserved cilantro and 1 tsp minced garlic, and cook until garlic is fragrant, about 30 seconds. Keep cilantro sauce warm until ready to use as baste for grilling shrimp. Divide sauce and reserve half of it for pouring over finished shrimp.

4. Prepare outdoor grill or stovetop griddle for high heat. Remove shrimp from marinade and place on grill. Discard marinade.

5. Grill kebabs 1½ minutes per side. Baste with cilantro sauce from stovetop every 30 seconds. Do not overcook or shrimp will be rubbery.

6. Remove shrimp from grill, transfer to plates, and pour reserved cilantro sauce over shrimp. Serve with juicy lime wedges on the side. Encourage your guests or family to squeeze juice from wedges over shrimp before eating.

Chef's Notes: Choosing between metal and wood skewers is a matter of personal preference. Wooden skewers burn if not soaked in water for at least 20 minutes before using, and metal skewers can burn YOU if not handled carefully after grilling. Be careful and take appropriate precautions no matter which skewers you choose to use.

Spicy Barbecue Shrimp

Ingredients

¼ cup coconut oil, melted

3 garlic cloves, minced

2 Tbsp lemon juice

⅛ tsp paprika

Cayenne pepper, to taste

Sea salt, to taste

2½ lbs shelled shrimp with tail left on

Lime wedges and parsley for garnish

Preparation

1. Add coconut oil, garlic, lemon juice, paprika, cayenne pepper, sea salt, and lemon juice to bowl, and whisk.

2. Preheat stovetop griddle to medium-high. While griddle is heating, coat shrimp with coconut oil preparation, using silicone basting brush. Place shrimp on griddle and grill 1½ minutes per side. Do not overcook or shrimp will be rubbery. Garnish shrimp with lime wedges and parsley. Encourage your guests or family to squeeze lime juice over shrimp before eating.

White Balsamic Mussels

SERVES 4

Ingredients

---

4 lbs fresh mussels

¼ cup white balsamic vinegar

1¾ cups chicken stock (page 243)

2 medium onions, chopped

5 garlic cloves, minced

⅓ cup of your favorite chopped fresh herbs (basil, cilantro, or mint work nicely)

6 Tbsp coconut oil

Preparation

1. In pot, combine vinegar, chicken stock, onions, and garlic. Bring to a boil, then reduce heat and simmer for 6 minutes.

2. Add mussels to pot, cover (preferably with glass lid, so that you can see them) and increase heat to medium-high, so that stock mixture boils. When all of the mussels have opened, remove them from heat and stir in herbs and coconut oil. Spoon into bowls and serve immediately with crab forks (small forks) to pick mussels out of their shells.

Be sure to purchase mussels the same day you will serve them. Store them on ice or in refrigerator until you're ready. When it's time to prepare them, place them in ice water and remove the "beard" or stringy membrane attached to most mussel shells. Some stores will debeard them for you upon request. Mussels should be clamped firmly shut. Discard any that are open, even a little. Typically, you will have to discard more than a few.

Lime and Garlic Scallops

SERVES 6

Ingredients

½ cup coconut oil

6 garlic cloves, minced

2 Tbsp lime or lemon juice

2 lbs large scallops

Sea salt and freshly ground black pepper, to taste

Fresh parsley or chives for garnish (optional)

Preparation

1. Heat non-stick skillet over medium heat and melt coconut oil. Add minced garlic and cook for one minute, until fragrant. Remove garlic to small bowl.
2. Add scallops and cook for about one minute on each side until they are firm and opaque.
3. Remove scallops from pan and set aside in a separate bowl. Remove skillet from heat and add lemon or lime juice and previously cooked garlic. Season to taste with salt and pepper. Plate scallops and pour lemony sauce over top. Garnish with parsley or chives, if desired.
4. You may also serve these scallops on a bed of steamed vegetables such as asparagus, broccoli, or cauliflower; or over a bunch of fresh greens.

{ Vegetarian Dishes }

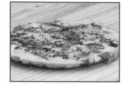

Ratatouille

SERVES 8

Ingredients

1¼ cups olive oil or tallow

4 large tomatoes (plum tomatoes are best, but any kind will do)

4 zucchini, cut into ¾ inch cubes

9 garlic cloves

2 lbs eggplant, cut into 1-inch cubes

2 large onions, sliced thinly

3 bell peppers of assorted colors cut into 1-inch cubes

1 cup fresh parsley, chopped

20 basil leaves, cut in half

Freshly ground black pepper and sea salt, to taste

Preparation

1. Remove skin from tomatoes if using fresh tomatoes. To do so, score an X on bottom of each one and blanch them in boiling water for a minute. Remove them from boiling water with slotted spoon and transfer to a bowl of cold water. When cool enough to handle, gently remove skin starting where you scored them.

2. Chop tomatoes and put them in 5–6 quart Dutch oven with about ¼ cup of cooking fat, parsley, basil leaves, and garlic. Cover pot and simmer for 30 minutes, stirring periodically, or until tomatoes break down and form sauce.

3. While tomatoes are simmering, sprinkle sea salt on eggplant cubes and put them in colander in kitchen sink. Fluid will seep from them and remove some of the bitterness from seeds. Leave them in colander while preparing other vegetables.

4. In non-stick skillet over medium heat, cook onions in another ¼ cup of cooking fat for 5–7 minutes or until translucent. Remove onions with slotted spoon and set aside in large bowl.

5. Add a little more cooking fat to skillet. Add bell peppers and sauté until crisp-tender. Remove with slotted spoon and add to bowl with onions.

6. Add a little more cooking fat to skillet. Add zucchini and sauté until crisp-tender. Remove and set aside with other vegetables.

7. Pat eggplant cubes dry, add them to skillet with a little more cooking fat. Sauté for about 7 minutes. Remove them from skillet and turn off the heat.

8. Once tomato preparation has simmered for at least 30 minutes, add all cooked vegetables in bowl, season generously with ground black pepper, cover and simmer for about another hour, until all they are very soft. Adjust seasoning as needed with salt and pepper.

9. Serve hot, warm, or cold, with chopped basil or chopped parsley as garnish.

Baba-Ghanoush

Ingredients

3 medium eggplants
2 garlic cloves, minced
2 Tbsp lemon or lime juice
1 tsp tahini
1 Tbsp olive oil
1 tsp cumin
Sea salt and freshly ground black pepper, to taste
Fresh parsley for garnish, optional

Preparation

1. Preheat oven to 400° F. Prick skin of eggplants several times with fork, place on cookie sheet or roasting pan and bake for 30–35 minutes.
2. Place roasted eggplants in bowl of ice water and soak until you can handle comfortably. Once cool, peel and cut it into chunks.
3. Place roasted eggplant pieces, garlic, lemon or lime juice, tahini, olive oil, and cumin in blender or food processor and blend until smooth. Season to taste with salt and pepper.
4. Cool in refrigerator and serve with extra olive oil on top and garnish with fresh parsley, if desired.
5. Baba-ghanoush is wonderful served with fresh vegetables for dipping.

Zucchini and Carrot Frittata

Ingredients

---

2 Tbsp coconut oil

1 cup carrots, chopped

2 medium zucchini, diced

1 bell pepper, sliced

8 large eggs

2 Tbsp fresh parsley for garnish (optional)

Sea salt and freshly ground black pepper, to taste

Preparation

1. Heat ovenproof non-stick skillet (cast iron is best) over medium heat. Add oil and carrots to skillet and cook until they are softened, about 7 minutes, stirring occasionally.

2. Turn oven to broil setting.

3. Add zucchini and bell pepper slices to skillet, and cook for 5 minutes, stirring occasionally.

4. While vegetables are cooking, crack eggs into bowl and whisk until frothy in order to make frittata as light and airy as possible.

5. Season egg mixture with salt and pepper, then whisk again. Add seasoned eggs to skillet with vegetables.

6. Reduce heat to low, and cook until edges are set, about 10 minutes.

7. Transfer skillet to oven and broil until golden, checking every 2 minutes. Remove from oven and cut into wedges. Serve warm.

Veggie Kebabs

SERVES 2

Ingredients

2-inch piece of ginger root, peeled

2 garlic cloves, minced

½ cup Paleo vinaigrette of choice (pages 190–205)

2 cups water

½ tsp red pepper flakes, to taste

1 Tbsp dried basil

1 Tbsp dried oregano

4 mushrooms (button or cremini)

1 zucchini, sliced thick

½ head of cauliflower, pulled apart into florets

1 red bell pepper, cut into large pieces

2 carrots, sliced thick

1 medium onion, quartered

Wooden or metal skewers

Preparation

1. Prepare marinade by blending ginger root, garlic, vinaigrette, water, pepper flakes, basil, and oregano in bowl, using whisk to combine thoroughly.

2. Place prepared vegetables in bowl and pour marinade over top. Toss well to coat. Place in refrigerator and marinate overnight.

3. If using wooden skewers, soak them in water for at least 15 minutes to avoid charring. Heat outdoor grill or indoor griddle to high heat. Oil cooking surface lightly, using coconut oil and silicone basting brush.

4. Skewer vegetables and place on grill. Cook, turning frequently, until vegetables are crisp-tender, about 10 minutes. Baste with marinade throughout grilling. Remove from grill and plate. Serve warm on or off skewer, as desired.

Chef's Notes: Choosing between metal and wood skewers is a matter of personal preference. Wooden skewers burn if not soaked in water for at least 20 minutes before using, and metal skewers can burn YOU if not handled carefully after grilling. Be careful and take appropriate precautions no matter which skewers you choose to use.

Stuffed Portobello

SERVES 2

Ingredients

4 large portobello mushroom caps
1 Tbsp olive oil
12 oz yellow fin tuna, canned in oil, drained
1 medium avocado, peeled and pit removed
⅛ tsp red pepper, ground
Sea salt, to taste
Fresh garlic or garlic powder, optional
Mixed-color peppercorns, optional

Preparation

1. Heat stovetop griddle or outside grill to medium-high heat. Rub outside of mushrooms with olive oil. Place mushrooms on grill or griddle, and grill for 2–3 minutes, just long enough to create grill marks and/or gently heat. Remove from cooking surface and set aside, keeping them warm.
2. Add remaining ingredients to bowl and mash with fork to combine. Stuff mushroom caps with ingredients and serve immediately to prevent avocado from darkening.
3. For a variation on the recipe, chop dried fruits and sprinkle over top of the mushrooms or incorporate into stuffing. Consider adding curry powder to stuffing for an Indian flavor, or add your favorite chopped nuts for some added crunch.

Chef's Note: You may use fresh tuna for this recipe instead of canned. Heat a non-stick skillet over medium-high heat with a little coconut oil. Place tuna in the hot skillet and sear both sides to desired doneness (about 1½ minutes on each side for medium doneness). Flake tuna with a fork before proceeding.

Cabbage and Apple Stir-Fry

SERVES 4–6

Ingredients

1–2 Tbsp coconut oil

1 large apple, cored and sliced

1½ lbs cabbage, shredded

1 medium onion, thinly sliced

1 red chili pepper, finely chopped

1 Tbsp fresh thyme, chopped

1 Tbsp apple cider vinegar

⅔ cup almonds, chopped (optional)

Preparation

1. Heat wok over medium-high heat with coconut oil. When hot, add apple slices and stir-fry for 1 minute. Remove from wok and set aside.

2. Add a little more coconut oil and onion to wok, and stir-fry for 1 minute. Add cabbage and stir-fry an additional 3 minutes.

3. Return apple slices to wok and add thyme and cider vinegar. Cover and allow to cook for one minute. Turn off burner, add almonds (if desired), and toss gently to mix. Serve immediately.

Chef's Note: Try red cabbage in this recipe for a beautiful dish chockful of antioxidants.

{ Confit and Pâté }

Duck Confit

SERVES 4

Ingredients

4 duck legs with thighs

4 duck wings

4 cups duck fat

3 Tbsp sea salt

4 garlic cloves, minced

1 medium onion, thinly sliced

6 sprigs thyme, each 4 inches long

3 sprigs rosemary, each 4 inches long

Freshly ground black pepper to taste

Preparation

1. Mix salt and pepper together until combined. Add minced garlic, sliced onion, thyme sprigs, and rosemary sprigs.
2. Using dish large enough to hold all duck pieces in single layer, sprinkle ⅓ of fresh herb mixture on bottom. Place duck pieces in dish, skin-side up.
3. Sprinkle salt and pepper and remaining ⅔ of herb mixture evenly on top of duck.
4. Cover and refrigerate for a minimum of 24 and a maximum of 48 hours.
5. Preheat oven to 225° F.
6. Rinse herbs and spices from duck and arrange in baking dish in tight single layer.
7. Melt duck fat and pour over duck, making sure it completely covers duck. Place baking dish in oven for 2–4 hours or until meat can easily be pulled from bone.
8. Pull meat from bone and place in storage container with melted duck fat. Store in refrigerator for up to 4 weeks.

Duck confit is a tasty addition to any meal; you can serve it at breakfast with poached eggs, for lunch with pear salad, or at dinner with oyster mushrooms, onions and carrots.

Carrot Confit

SERVES 4

Ingredients

2 lbs carrots

Zest of 2 lemons or limes

Juice of 2 lemons or limes

4 garlic cloves, minced

2 sprigs German thyme or lemon thyme, each 4 inches long

1 cup duck fat, melted (or coconut oil, tallow or lard)

Preparation

1. Preheat oven to 275° F.
2. Leave carrots whole or cut them into pieces that will fit easily in baking dish.
3. In separate bowl, mix zest, juice, garlic, thyme, and melted fat together, and pour over carrots. Make sure they are completely covered. Place dish in oven for approximately 2 hours or until they have completely softened.
4. Remove carrots from oven and place in non-stick skillet over medium-high heat. Brown until the exterior is crispy. Serve warm as side with any main course.

Cinnamon Chicken Liver Pâté

SERVES 2

Ingredients

3 bacon slices (no preservatives and naturally seasoned), chopped
½ lb chicken livers
1 medium onion, diced
1 garlic clove, minced
¾ cup coconut oil
4 Tbsp fresh parsley, chopped
3 Tbsp white balsamic vinegar
⅛ tsp ground cinnamon
Sea salt and freshly ground black pepper, to taste

Preparation

1. Heat non-stick skillet to medium-high heat and cook bacon for about 3 minutes, flipping occasionally. Add onion, garlic, and ¼ cup of coconut oil to skillet and cook for 4 minutes, stirring occasionally.
2. While onions are cooking, cut white stringy membrane out of chicken livers.
3. Add livers and a little more cooking fat to skillet, and cook for 7 minutes, or until cooked through. Add white balsamic vinegar, parsley, salt, pepper, and cinnamon. Toss to coat livers.
4. Remove skillet from heat and pour mixture into blender or food processor, and blend or process until smooth. Spoon mixture into serving dish.
5. Pour remaining cooking fat (melted) over pâté evenly.
6. Cover and put in refrigerator to cool until fat hardens. Before serving, remove hardened layer of fat, if desired. Serve cool.

Holiday Chicken and Pork Pâté

SERVES 10

Ingredients

1 cup animal fat (duck, tallow, or even coconut oil will work)

2½ lb chicken livers

1 medium pork heart (may substitute beef heart)

2 large onions, diced

1 garlic clove, minced

1 cup fresh basil, chopped

5 tsp ground cinnamon

4 Tbsp apple cider vinegar

1½ cup fresh or frozen cranberries, divided

Salt and freshly ground black pepper, to taste

Preparation

1. Place ½ cup animal fat in Dutch oven over medium-high heat. Once it melts, add onions and sauté for 5–7 minutes, or until onions are translucent. Add garlic and sauté for 30 seconds.
2. While onions are cooking, cut white stringy membrane out of chicken livers.
3. Reduce heat to medium. Add liver and heart to Dutch oven and cook 7–10 minutes, or until liver and heart are cooked through. Add a little salt and pepper, to taste.
4. Toss together vinegar, basil, and half the fresh or thawed frozen cranberries.

Perform the following steps in batches, depending upon the size of your blender or food processer:

1. Spoon mixture into blender or food processor. Add cinnamon and blend or process until smooth. Remove from blender or food processor and place in bowl.
2. Halve each of the remaining cranberries with paring knife.
3. Add cranberries to pâté and gently mix. Taste and adjust seasonings as necessary with salt, pepper, and cinnamon.
4. Melt remaining duck fat in saucepan and pour over top of pâté.
5. Cover bowl and place in refrigerator to chill and allow fat to harden for approximately 2 hours.

{ Desserts }

Lime Coconut Candy

MAKES 28 CANDIES

Ingredients

1 cup coconut cream concentrate

½ cup honey

Zest of one lime

Juice of one lime

1 cup coconut flakes, unsweetened (optional)

½ tsp vanilla extract (optional)

Preparation

1. In non-stick saucepan, over medium-high heat, warm coconut cream until smooth and has thick but stir-able consistency. Transfer to mixing bowl and immediately add remaining ingredients, stirring well to combine.

2. Once mixture has cooled and stiffened enough to handle (place bowl in refrigerator if necessary), use tablespoon to spoon out candy mixture and form into balls. Roll balls in dried coconut for added crunchy texture. Place coconut balls on cookie sheet and put in freezer until firm.

3. A second method is to omit coconut flakes and place candy mixture in candy molds and freeze. Remove from freezer once firm and serve immediately.

4. Candies will keep in freezer in airtight container for up to 30 days.

Chef's Note: The quantity of lime juice and zest you use is entirely dependent on how much lime flavor you like. I prefer the juice and zest of 4 limes. You may use lemons in place of limes, and use 2-3 for juice and zest. For another variation in flavor and appearance, toast the shredded coconut before rolling the candy balls in it.

ChocoCherry Cookie Dough Truffles

MAKES 32 TRUFFLES

Ingredients

1¼ cups almond flour	¼ cup coconut oil, melted
¼ tsp sea salt	1½ tsp vanilla extract
¼ cup agave nectar or honey	¼ cup cherries, dried, unsweetened

Chocolate Candy Exterior

⅔ cup dairy-free dark chocolate chips	1½ Tbsp coconut oil

Preparation

1. Mix almond flour, salt, and honey in bowl.
2. In smaller bowl, mix remaining wet ingredients. Pour wet mixture into flour mixture, and stir well to combine. Fold in dried cherries.
3. Using tablespoon, spoon out dough and roll into 1-inch balls. Place on plate or lined cookie sheet. Place in freezer for 30 minutes to set.

Chocolate Candy Exterior:

1. In double boiler or saucepan over simmering water, melt chocolate chips and coconut oil. Stir well to combine.
2. Remove chocolate candy coating from heat. Remove cookie dough from freezer and insert toothpick in center of dough ball. One at a time, dip each ball into chocolate, roll to coat it, and return to plate or cookie sheet.
3. Place balls back in freezer for 10 minutes to allow chocolate to harden.
4. Truffles will keep in airtight container in refrigerator for up to 2 weeks or in freezer for up to 30 days.

Chef's Note: The amount of honey can be adjusted a little upward or downward to get the level of sweetness desired. You may substitute any dried fruit or more dairy-free chocolate chips for the cherries in this recipe. Be sure to use fruit that is artificial-preservative free.

Chocolate Chip Cookies

MAKES 20 COOKIES

Ingredients

1 cup almond butter

1 large egg

¼ cup cacao powder

¼ cup dairy-free chocolate chips

2 tsp vanilla extract

¼ cup honey

Preparation

1. Preheat oven to 350° F.
2. Combine all ingredients in mixing bowl and stir well until combined.
3. Using tablespoon, drop cookie dough onto parchment paper-lined (or silicone-lined) baking sheet. Using back of large spoon, slightly flatten cookies.
4. Place cookies in oven and bake until firm to the touch, 10–12 minutes. For softer cookies, bake them only 8–10 minutes.

Chef's Note: You can make your own almond butter by placing almonds and a few drops of almond oil in the food processor and processing until a desired consistency. If cookies are too sweet for your palate, decrease the amount of honey by half.

Cinnamon Carrot Cookies

MAKES 20 COOKIES

Ingredients

2 cups carrots, diced

2 cups roasted almonds, unsalted

1 cup coconut flakes, unsweetened

½ tsp ground cinnamon

⅛ tsp ground coriander

2 tsp vanilla extract

2 tsp coconut oil, melted

2 Tbsp honey (optional)

3 large eggs, lightly beaten

Preparation

1. Preheat oven to 350° F.
2. Place carrots, almonds, dried coconut, cinnamon, coriander, vanilla extract, coconut oil, and honey in food processor and pulse until mixture is well combined, and carrots and almonds are in small chunks.
3. Remove cookie dough from food processor using flexible spatula and place in mixing bowl. Add eggs to cookie dough and mix well until dough is an even consistency.
4. Using ¼-cup measuring cup, dip out dough and use your hand to shape into cookie patties. Place cookies on parchment paper-lined or silicone-lined cookie sheet.
5. Place cookies in oven and bake for 20–30 minutes, or until firm to the touch.

Chef's Note: For softer cookies, shorten cooking time. For flavor variation, try adding a dash of nutmeg and/or ⅛ cup unsweetened raisins

Almond Apple Cookies

Makes 20 cookies

Ingredients

---

2 cups apples, cored and chopped

2 cups roasted almonds, unsalted

1 cup shredded coconut, unsweetened

2 Tbsp ground cinnamon

2 tsp vanilla extract

2 tsp coconut oil, melted and cooled slightly

3 large eggs, lightly beaten

Preparation

1. Preheat oven to 350° F.
2. Leave apple skins on for additional vitamins and nutrients. Combine apples, almonds, coconut, cinnamon, vanilla extract, and coconut oil in food processor and pulse until well combined, and apples and almonds are in small chunks.
3. Remove cookie dough from food processor using flexible spatula and place in mixing bowl. Add eggs to cookie dough and mix well until dough is an even consistency.
4. Using ¼-cup measuring cup, dip out dough and use your hand to shape into cookie patties. Place cookies on parchment paper-lined or silicone-lined cookie sheet.
5. Place cookies in oven and bake until firm to the touch: 20–25 minutes (check after 15 minutes). For softer cookies, reduce cooking time.

Pistachio Pudding

Ingredients

1 cup pistachio nuts, unsalted, shelled	¼ cup water, for soaking nuts
¼ cup agave nectar or honey	½ tsp sea salt
3 medium avocados, peeled and pitted	½ tsp fresh lemon juice
1 Tbsp water	2 Tbsp pistachios, chopped, for topping

Preparation

1. Soak shelled pistachios in water for 2–3 hours. Drain and rinse.
2. Using high speed blender, Vita-Mix, or food processor, purée pistachios with honey/nectar and 1 Tbsp water on high until smooth paste is formed. It could take up to 10 minutes to form nut paste, so make sure you are using blender/processor with strong motor. There may be small chunks still in paste, which is good for variation in texture. Place pistachio paste and unpeeled avocados in fridge overnight or at least 4 hours. (If you have already peeled the avocados, place them in a bag and add some lemon juice to keep them from browning.)
3. After chilling, halve avocado, remove pit, and flesh from peel. Add avocado flesh, salt, and lemon juice to nut paste and place in blender or food processor. Blend/process on high until avocado and nut paste is well blended and smooth. You will need to stop blending periodically to scrape down sides using spatula. If necessary, add water and/or lemon juice to thin out pudding mix.
4. Test small quantity for texture and taste. Texture should be similar to that of mousse with small bits of crunchy pistachios. You will not taste the citrus juice, which is added just to preserve color. Avocados oxidize and darken when exposed to oxygen. It's not dangerous, just not attractive.
5. Remove pudding from blender, and chill in refrigerator for 4 hours before serving. Garnish with additional chopped pistachios when plated, if desired.

Apple Crisp

Ingredients

2 cups almond flour

½ tsp sea salt

1 tsp ground cinnamon

¼ tsp ground coriander

⅛ tsp nutmeg

⅓ cup coconut oil, melted

¼ cup agave nectar or honey

1 Tbsp vanilla extract

4 large apples, peeled and cored

Preparation

1. Preheat oven to 350° F. Grease 2-quart glassbaking dish with coconut oil, and set aside.

2. Peel, core, and slice each apple into 8 equally sized slices. Place them in baking dish and set it aside.

3. In bowl, mix almond flour, sea salt, cinnamon, coriander, and nutmeg. Whisk until well combined.

4. In smaller bowl, add agave or honey, melted coconut oil, and vanilla, and whisk until well combined. Stir wet mixture into dry and combine thoroughly. Top apple slices with this mixture.

5. Cover baking dish with foil or lid and place it in oven. Bake for 40–50 minutes until bubbly and apples are starting to get translucent. Remove cover and bake for 5–10 more minutes, until crisp topping browns, but be careful not to burn it! Serve warm.

Blueberry Citrus Pound Cake

MAKES 8–10 SLICES

Ingredients

1 cup + 2 Tbsp almond flour

¼ cup + 2 Tbsp coconut flour, sifted

¼ cup agave nectar

¼ tsp salt

1½ tsp baking powder

1½ tsp lemon extract (optional)

1½ tsp vanilla extract

1 Tbsp water

3 large eggs

1½ cups blueberries, canned, rinsed, and drained

Coconut oil, solid, for greasing loaf pan

Preparation

1. Preheat oven to 350° F. Grease inside of loaf pan with coconut oil.
2. In large bowl, combine almond and coconut flours, salt, and baking powder. Whisk to combine and aerate.
3. In second bowl, combine lemon extract (if using), vanilla extract, agave nectar, eggs and water. Mix well. Add wet ingredients to dry, and mix until uniformly moist. Fold in blueberries.
4. Bake for 35 minutes or until toothpick inserted in center of loaf comes out clean. Cool on rack before slicing. Slice only as much as you intend to serve. Leave loaf whole to preserve moistness.

Chef Note: Do not substitute lemon juice for lemon extract. You may omit it from the recipe if necessary, or replace it with grated lemon zest.

Red Velvet Loaf

MAKES 8–10 SLICES

Ingredients

---

2 large (apple sized) or 3 medium beets, peeled and coarsely chopped
6 large eggs
¼ tsp sea salt
½ cup coconut milk
½ cup coconut flour, sifted
1 cup almond flour
1½ cup cacao powder
1 tsp vanilla extract
½ tsp cinnamon
1 cup honey
Coconut fat, solid, for greasing loaf pan

Preparation

1. Preheat oven to 375° F. Grease loaf pan with solid coconut oil.
2. Peel and cut beets into chunks. Pressure-cook beets until soft according to instructions on your cooker, or cook on stovetop over medium-high heat in enough water to cover until soft. Drain beets and place them in bowl of ice to cool quickly.
3. Place drained, cooled beets and eggs in food processor, and process until very smooth. Add remaining recipe ingredients to beet mixture in food processor and pulse until smooth.
4. Pour batter into greased loaf pan. Place in oven and bake until toothpick inserted in center comes out clean, 25–30 minutes.
5. Remove from oven and cool on rack for 5 minutes before removing from pan. Slice only as much as you intend to serve. Leave loaf whole to preserve moistness.

Cookie Cupcakes with Strawberry Cream Frosting

Ingredients

Cookie Cupcakes:

2 oz dairy-free chocolate

2 Tbsp coconut oil, plus some for
  greasing tins

2 Tbsp honey

3 Tbsp cacao powder

1 large egg

1 tsp vanilla extract

2 cups almond flour

1 Tbsp coconut flour, sifted

½ tsp baking soda

¼ tsp sea salt

Strawberry Cream Frosting:

2 cups chopped strawberries,
  fresh or frozen

¼ cup honey

1 cup coconut milk, unsweetened

½ cup coconut cream concentrate

Preparation
Cupcakes

1. Preheat oven to 325° F. Grease mini muffin tin very well with solid coconut oil.
2. Using double boiler or saucepan over simmering water, melt together chocolate, coconut oil, honey, and cacao powder. Stir often to combine. Once melted, remove from heat and cool.
3. Crack egg in large bowl and whisk with vanilla. Gradually add cooled chocolate mixture to egg, stirring to combine. Do not mix egg and chocolate mixture while it is hot or egg will cook. Add almond flour, coconut flour, baking soda, and salt to bowl, and stir to combine.
4. Form cupcake dough into 24 balls (approximately 1 tablespoon of dough each). Press into mini muffin tins and form well in center.
5. Bake for 10–12 minutes. Cool for 5 minutes in pan and remove from tins. You can also use a baking sheet, just remember to form the wells in the center.

Strawberry Cream Frosting:

1. In sturdy food processor, purée strawberries. Transfer strawberry purée to saucepan and bring to medium heat. Add honey to saucepan and bring to a gentle boil. Gently boil for 15 minutes until reduced and slightly thickened. Remove from heat and cool to room temperature.

2. Add coconut cream and coconut milk to puréed strawberries and mix thoroughly. If necessary, return saucepan to the heat and warm through, stirring constantly. Remove strawberry mixture from saucepan and place in bowl in refrigerator. Chill until set.

3. Scoop or pipe strawberry cream onto cookie cupcakes and drizzle with melted chocolate, if desired.

Zucchini Brownies

Ingredients

1 cup almond butter

⅓ cup honey

1 large egg

1 tsp baking soda

1 tsp vanilla extract

1 tsp ground cinnamon

1 cup dairy-free dark chocolate chips

2 Tbsp dairy-free chocolate chips (for topping)

1½ cup zucchini, shredded

Coconut oil, solid, for greasing pan

Preparation

1. Preheat oven to 350° F. Grease a 9" x 9" baking dish with coconut oil.
2. In medium bowl, combine almond butter, honey, egg, vanilla extract, baking soda, and cinnamon using electric beater until blended. Batter will be very thick.
3. Stir in zucchini and chocolate chips. Batter will thin out a little due to moisture in zucchini.
4. Pour or spoon batter into prepared pan, sprinkle with chocolate chips for topping, and bake for 35–45 minutes or until toothpick comes out clean when inserted in center.
5. Place baking dish on wire rack and cool before cutting into individual brownies. Store in airtight container in refrigerator. Enjoy at room temperature, or microwave for 10 seconds for warm brownie.

Chef's Note: You may peel the zucchini before grating it if you don't want small bits of green skin visible in the brownies. The chocolate chips will sink to the bottom except for the chips you sprinkled on top just before baking. Try adding a little freshly grated nutmeg for an additional flavor kick.

Coconut Cream Pie

Ingredients

Crust

¾ cup coconut flour, sifted

½ cup coconut flakes, unsweetened

3 large eggs

¼ cup coconut oil, melted

2 Tbsp coconut crystals

¼ tsp sea salt

¼ tsp baking soda

1 tsp vanilla extract

2 Tbsp cold water (more if needed)

2 oz dark chocolate (85% or higher cacao) or dairy-free chocolate

Filling

4 large egg yolks

3¼ cups coconut milk

7 oz creamed coconut

⅔ cup coconut crystals

1 tsp vanilla extract

¼ tsp sea salt

9 Tbsp arrowroot powder

Whipped Topping (optional)

1 cup coconut whipping cream (or heavy whipping cream for non-paleo appetites)

¼ cup coconut crystals

1 tsp vanilla extract, to taste (optional)

Garnish

½ cup coconut flakes, unsweetened

Dark chocolate shavings (85% or higher cacao) or dairy-free chocolate

Preparation

1. Place coconut flour and coconut flakes into food processor and pulse until combined. In separate bowl, whisk together eggs, coconut oil, coconut crystals, sea salt, baking soda, and vanilla extract.

2. Add wet ingredients to food processor, and pulse until it forms crumbly dough. Slowly add water until dough comes together and appears moist but not too sticky.

3. Spread dough into 9-inch pie dish and bake at 325°F for approximately 15 minutes, or until golden brown. Melt dark chocolate in microwave double boiler.

4. Once pie shell is completely cooled, use pastry brush to coat it with melted chocolate. Place coated pie shell in refrigerator to harden.

5. Prepare an ice bath and set it aside. In bowl, lightly whisk egg yolks and set aside. In saucepan, combine coconut milk, creamed coconut, coconut crystals, vanilla extract, and salt. Bring to a simmer and cook, whisking constantly, for about 10 minutes. You want to cook some of the liquid out of the coconut milk, so that it concentrates the flavor and thickens a bit.

6. Whisk a quarter of hot coconut milk mixture into egg yolks, then gradually whisk in remaining coconut milk mixture. Pour into clean saucepan and cook over medium-high heat, whisking constantly, until custard is thicker and bubbles appear in center, about 10 minutes. Transfer to medium bowl and set in ice bath. Whisk it occasionally while it cools off (a total of 30–40 minutes). Sift in arrowroot powder, and whisk until combined and somewhat thicker (it will continue to thicken in refrigerator).

7. Place layer of plastic wrap onto surface of coconut mixture to prevent skin from forming, then place bowl in refrigerator. Filling can be kept in refrigerator, covered with plastic wrap, for up to 24 hours.

8. Place coconut flakes on rimmed baking sheet and bake until lightly golden brown. Set aside.

9. Fill cooled crust with cooled custard, and spread evenly with spatula.

10. Refrigerate finished coconut cream pie for at least 3 hours. Garnish with toasted coconut flakes and some grated dark chocolate just before serving. Pie can be made in advance and refrigerated for up to 3 days. The entire recipe is gluten, dairy, and nut free.

Continued on next page

Continued from previous page

Coconut Whipped Topping:
1. Place can of coconut milk in refrigerator until well-chilled. (2–3 hours or overnight.)
2. Open can of coconut milk. There will be firm, waxy layer on top. Scoop out this firm layer of coconut cream that has solidified at top of can.
3. Stop as soon as you reach water at bottom of can; don't include anything but solid cream. (You can save the water for a smoothie recipe, though).
4. Place coconut cream in bowl of stand mixer in large bowl. Add coconut crystals and vanilla, if desired.
5. Turn your mixer or hand beater to high speed, and whip coconut cream for 3–5 minutes. Whip until it becomes fluffy and light, with soft peaks. Use it as a topping and then garnish with toasted coconut and grated dark chocolate just before serving.

No Bake Key Lime Pie

Ingredients

Crust:

1 cup macadamia nuts

1 cup coconut flakes, unsweetened

5 medjool dates, pitted

1 Tbsp coconut oil

Filling:

6 medium avocados

1½ cup lime juice (approximately 3 limes)

½ cup coconut oil, melted

1 cup honey

⅔ cup coconut cream

Preparation

Crust:

1. Blend all ingredients in food processor and press firmly into pop-out cake tin.

Filling:

1. Blend filling ingredients in food processor and spread on top of crust base.

2. Refrigerate for at least 30 minutes and serve once completely cooled.

Molten Lava Cakes

MAKES 4 INDIVIDUAL CAKES

Ingredients

4 oz dairy-free chocolate	2 Tbsp honey
4 Tbsp coconut oil	1 tsp coconut flour
2 large eggs	2 tsp cacao powder
½ tsp vanilla extract	Coconut oil for greasing muffin tins
⅛ tsp sea salt	Coconut flour for flouring muffin tins

Preparation

1. Preheat oven to 375° F. Grease and flour 6 standard muffin tins with coconut oil and coconut flour.
2. In double boiler, melt chocolate and coconut oil together until smooth, stirring occasionally. You can also use microwave, stirring every 30 seconds.
3. In small bowl, beat eggs, vanilla extract, salt, and honey with hand mixer until light and frothy, about 5 minutes.
4. Pour egg mixture over chocolate. Sift cacao and coconut flour over top. Then gently fold all ingredients together with plastic or silicone spatula.
5. Pour batter into prepared muffin tins until they are about halfway full. Place oven and bake for 11–12 minutes.
6. Remove from oven and serve immediately. Enjoy!

Chef's Note: To prepare these cakes in advance, chill the unbaked cakes in the tins in the refrigerator until 45 minutes before baking. Remove from the refrigerator and bring to room temperature. Place the cakes in a preheated oven and bake as instructed. Four-ounce ceramic ramekins may be used in place of muffin tins.

Banana Layer Cake

MAKES 6 SERVINGS

Ingredients

2 cups almond butter	1 tsp vanilla extract	1 tsp baking soda
4 medium bananas	2 tsp apple cider vinegar	½ tsp sea salt
4 large eggs, 1 reserved whole, the rest mashed	2 Tbsp ghee or coconut oil, melted	4 Tbsp coconut flour, sifted
4 Tbsp honey	1 tsp cinnamon	

Coconut Whipped Topping

One 15-ounce can full-fat coconut milk	1 tsp vanilla, to taste (optional)
¼ cup coconut crystals	

Preparation

1. Place can of coconut milk in refrigerator and leave it there until well-chilled (2–3 hours or overnight) for coconut whipped topping.
2. Preheat oven to 350° F.
3. Generously oil 13" x 9" cake pan. Line bottom with unbleached parchment paper.
4. Mix all dry ingredients (last 4) together in bowl.
5. In separate bowl, mix all wet ingredients (first 6). Combine dry and wet ingredients together and mix until combined.
6. Pour batter into prepared cake pan, spread evenly with spatula, and bake for 40 minutes. When done, cake should have risen slightly and should look golden brown.
7. Let cool in pan for 15 minutes before cutting. Meanwhile, slice reserved banana. Cut cake into squares and layer with coconut whipped cream and sliced bananas.

Coconut Whipped Topping

1. Remove coconut milk from refrigerator and open can. There will be a firm, waxy layer on top. Scoop out this firm layer of coconut cream that has solidified at top

of can. Stop as soon as you reach water at bottom of can; don't include anything but solid cream. (You can save the water for a smoothie recipe.)

2. Place coconut cream in bowl of stand mixer or in large bowl. Add coconut crystals and vanilla, if using. Turn your mixer or hand beater to high speed, and whip coconut cream for 3–5 minutes. Whip until it becomes fluffy and light, with soft peaks.

Chef's Note: This recipe is great to make muffins or bread as well. I would suggest 40–60 minutes for a loaf of bread (one recipe makes 2 small loaves). Muffins can take from 10–30 minutes depending on their size (one recipe makes lots of muffins).

{ Vinaigrettes and Dressings }

{ Salad Dressings and Vinaigrettes }

Vinaigrettes can be defined as a combination of an acid, usually vinegar or citrus juice, with spices and herbs and oil. Dijon mustard is often added to helpkeep all ingredients in solution. The order of ingredient addition is important. For example, always add oil as the last ingredient. That way any ingredients that need to dissolve in the vinegar will do so before adding the oil, which inhibits dissolution. Oil is typically added to the vinegar or citrus juice in a slow drizzle while whisking the liquid constantly. Naturally, you may also use a blender or food processor if you prefer.

Last but not least, always wait to add dressing to your salad just before serving, unless otherwise stated, or your salad greens will get soggy.

Lemon Vinaigrette

SERVES 4

Ingredients

3 Tbsp lime or lemon juice

½ tsp Dijon mustard (optional: add more if necessary to keep all ingredients in solution)

⅛ teaspoon dried lemon thyme (optional)

Sea salt and freshly ground black pepper, to taste

6 Tbsp olive oil

Preparation

1. Add lemon or lime juice to bowl with mustard, salt, and pepper, and whisk to combine. Drizzle oil in, whisking all the while. Adjust seasoning and mustard as necessary for flavor and consistency. Store in refrigerator in container with tight-fitting lid for up to 5 days. Bring to room temperature and shake well before serving.

Chef's Note: Some folks prefer more acid and less oil. Experiment with the ratios to create the flavor and consistency desired.

Balsamic Vinaigrette

Serves 6

Ingredients

¾ cup balsamic vinegar

1 garlic clove, minced

1 tsp dried oregano or basil

½ tsp onion powder or 1 tsp dried onion, minced

1 Tbsp Dijon mustard, (optional: add more if necessary to keep all ingredients
   in solution)

Sea salt and freshly ground black pepper, to taste

¾ cup olive oil

Preparation

1. Place vinegar, garlic, oregano or basil, onion, salt and pepper with Dijon mustard in bowl. Whisk to combine. Drizzle olive oil into bowl, whisking all the while.
2. Store in refrigerator in container with tight-fitting lid for up to 5 days. Bring to room temperature and shake well before serving.

Chef's Note: Balsamic is "sweeter" than most vinegars and an important ingredient in many classic and modern Italian and fusion recipes. Balsamic vinaigrette is a great marinade for meats, a fabulous drizzle for vegetables, and of course, a classic Italian salad dressing.

Tomato Vinaigrette

Ingredients

½ cup Paleo Lemon Vinaigrette (page 190)

4 oz cherry tomatoes

1 garlic clove, minced

¼ tsp onion powder

Preparation

1. Add all ingredients to blender or food processor, and process to smooth purée. Thin with a little water, if desired. Serve immediately.

2. Store in refrigerator for up to 5 days in container with tight-fitting lid. Bring to room temperature and shake well before serving.

Sauce Vierge

SERVES 8

Ingredients

1 garlic clove, minced
1 shallot, minced
7 Tbsp olive oil
½ cup tomatoes, peeled and finely diced
Juice of one lemon
1 tsp fresh basil, chopped
Sea salt

Preparation

1. In non-stick saucepan, bring olive oil, garlic, and shallot to medium-high heat and sauté for 30 seconds. Immediately add tomatoes and simmer for 5 minutes. Add basil and lemon juice, and mix well. Season sauce with sea salt, to taste. Serve sauce warm.

2. Store in refrigerator for up to 5 days in container with tight-fitting lid. Warm sauce in microwave and shake well before serving.

> **Chef's Note:** Sauce Vierge is commonly known as "virgin" sauce. It's served warm and is very pleasing to the palate. Try serving it drizzled over warm vegetables, fish, poultry, and seafood.

Caesar Dressing

Ingredients

1 Tbsp lemon juice

2 Tbsp Paleo Mayonnaise (page 211)

½ cup olive oil

6 garlic cloves, minced

1 Tbsp Dijon mustard

1 or 2 minced anchovy fillets, to taste

Sea salt and freshly ground black pepper, to taste

Preparation

1. Place lemon juice, garlic, anchovies, and mustard in food processor and blend to combine. Add mayonnaise and blend again. Drizzle olive oil in and continue to process until emulsified. Taste and adjust seasoning with salt, pepper, and lemon juice. Serve immediately.

2. Store in refrigerator for up to 5 days in container with tight-fitting lid. Bring to room temperature and shake well before serving.

Chef's Note: Use ⅛ tsp (or more) fish sauce in place of anchovies if you keep some on hand for Asian dishes and for a slight twist in the flavor.

Raspberry-Pecan Vinaigrette

Ingredients

3 Tbsp raspberry vinegar

½ tsp Dijon mustard (optional)

6 Tbsp walnut oil

2 Tbsp chopped pecans

Sea salt and freshly ground black pepper, to taste

Preparation

1. Place vinegar, mustard, salt and pepper in bowl and whisk to combine. Drizzle walnut oil into vinegar mixture, whisking constantly. Add pecans and mix well. Serve immediately.

2. Store in refrigerator for up to 5 days in container with tight-fitting lid. Bring to room temperature and shake well before serving.

Chef's Note: If you prefer not to purchase raspberry vinegar, you can make your own by placing ¼ cup of raspberries in 1 cup of vinegar. Mash the raspberries with a fork, and place in the refrigerator for 48 hours. Strain off the raspberries and reserve the vinegar. It can be stored in the refrigerator for up to 30 days.

Orange and Rosemary Vinaigrette

SERVES 4

Ingredients

---

3 Tbsp fresh lime or lemon juice

½ tsp Dijon mustard, optional

6 Tbsp olive oil

Grated zest and juice of 1 orange

1 tsp fresh rosemary, chopped

Sea salt and freshly ground black pepper, to taste

Preparation

1. Whisk together lime or lemon juice with mustard (if using), and zest and juice of orange. Add 1 tsp of chopped fresh rosemary. Place in refrigerator overnight to "infuse" orange flavor. Bring to room temperature and shake well before serving.

Ginger Vinaigrette

SERVES 4

Ingredients

---

3 Tbsp rice vinegar

1 inch piece of ginger root, peeled and finely grated

5 Tbsp olive oil

1 Tbsp sesame oil

Sea salt and freshly ground black pepper, to taste

Preparation

1. Whisk together grated ginger and rice vinegar in bowl. Drizzle in olive oil and sesame oil, whisking all the while. Season vinaigrette with salt and pepper to taste.

2. Store in refrigerator for up to 5 days in container with tight-fitting lid. Bring to room temperature and shake well before serving.

> **Chef's Note:** This vinaigrette is a great addition to any salad accompanying an Asian meal. Bitter greens and roasted beet salads are particularly good pairings.

Roasted Chili Dressing

SERVES 5

Ingredients

3 red chili peppers

6 Tbsp olive oil

3½ Tbsp lemon juice or lime juice

¼ cup fresh mint or basil, packed

Sea salt and freshly ground black
pepper, to taste

Preparation

Chili Roasting Method #1: Oven Preparation

1. Prick chilies with tip of knife, so that they don't explode while roasting. Place them under broiler until well roasted and their skin is completely charred.

Chili Roasting Method #2: Griddle Preparation

1. Heat cast iron or heavy-bottomed griddle over high heat on stovetop. Place chili peppers on griddle and place heavy pot on top of them. Roast until skin is charred, flipping once.

Chili Roasting Method #3: Flame Preparation

1. Using tongs, hold chili peppers close to flame of gas stove until charred.
2. When roasted, put on plate and immediately cover them with plastic wrap for 2 minutes to steam skins loose. Peel, open with knife, and remove seeds. Finely chop remaining flesh. Add chili peppers to bowl with lemon juice and mint or basil, then drizzle in olive oil, whisking all the while. Season to taste with salt and pepper. Whisk again to mix well.
3. Store in refrigerator for up to 5 days in container with tight-fitting lid. Bring to room temperature and shake well before serving.

Chef's Note: This is a dressing with a bold taste, so it will go well with bold salads featuring strong herbs or root vegetables.

{ Condiments }

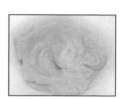

Mayonnaise

Ingredients

2 large egg yolks
1 tsp Paleo Mustard (optional, page 216)
3 tsp lemon juice
½ cup olive oil
½ cup coconut oil, melted

Preparation

1. Place egg yolks in bowl (or blender/food processor) with mustard (optional) and 1 tsp lemon juice. Whisk, blend or process, drizzling both oils in very slowly, until stable emulsion forms. If you add oil too quickly, emulsion will "break" and you cannot reverse it. Discard and start over.
2. When all of oil is incorporated and mayonnaise is thick, add remaining lemon juice and season to taste with salt and pepper.
3. Refrigerate leftover mayonnaise and use within 24 hours.

Chef's Note: Create flavored mayonnaise by adding herbs, spices, or even lacto-fermented cucumber relish or horseradish (pages 220, 228).

Do not substitute coconut oil for olive oil in this recipe or it will become too hard in the refrigerator. If you decide to use only olive oil in the recipe, use a light or mild-flavored variety to keep the mayonnaise flavor palatable for most people.

Mild Ketchup

Ingredients

6 oz tomato paste

2 Tbsp vinegar, lemon or lime juice

¼ tsp dry mustard

⅓ cup water

¼ tsp cinnamon

¼ tsp sea salt

1 pinch ground cloves

1 pinch ground allspice

⅛ tsp ground red pepper (optional)

Preparation

1. Combine all ingredients in bowl and whisk to combine. Place in refrigerator overnight to allow flavors to bloom. Serve cold or allow required quantity to come to room temperature before serving.

Robust Ketchup

YIELDS ABOUT 2 CUPS

Ingredients

---

2 lbs fresh plum tomatoes, chopped

1 large onion, finely diced

½ medium fennel bulb, finely chopped

1 celery stick, cut into cubes

1 inch piece of ginger root, peeled and minced

2 garlic cloves, minced

½ red chili pepper, seeded and finely chopped

1 tsp olive oil

1 cup fresh basil, chopped

1 Tbsp ground coriander seeds

1 tsp freshly ground black pepper

¾ cup + 2 Tbsp balsamic or apple cider vinegar

Sea salt, to taste

Preparation

1. Heat olive oil in non-stick skillet over medium heat with onion, fennel, celery, ginger, chili pepper, basil, coriander garlic, salt and pepper.

2. Sauté for about 10–12 minutes, or until vegetables are softened. Add 1½ cups of water and chopped tomatoes to skillet. Simmer gently until liquid reduces by half. Pour sauce into blender or food processor, and process until smooth. Strain sauce through sieve into new or cleaned saucepan and add vinegar.

3. Simmer again until thickened to desired consistency. Adjust seasoning to taste. Place saucepan on rack and cool for 10 minutes. Add ketchup to container without lid in refrigerator to cool completely. Cover with tight-fitting lid once cool and store for up to 30 days in refrigerator. Ketchup can be stored up to 6 months in a cool dark place when "canned" via proper food preservation methods.

Mustard

This is a basic recipe that will not have the typical consistency of mustard. It's thinner than you would expect but packed with flavor. Use it judiciously! Add herbs and spices or horseradish to vary the flavor. Store in a glass jar with a tight-fitting lid for up to one year in the refrigerator.

YIELDS ABOUT ½ CUP

Ingredients

½ cup mustard powder
¼ cup water
¼ cup white wine vinegar
Sea salt, to taste

Preparation

1. Combine mustard powder, water, and vinegar in bowl and whisk. Let stand for 30 minutes before using. Add sea salt, to taste. Use small quantities of the finished product brushed on bread for sandwiches and as an ingredient for other recipes in this book.

Dijon Style Mustard

Ingredients

¼ cup yellow mustard seeds

¼ cup brown mustard seeds

1 cup white balsamic vinegar

4 tsp mustard powder

¼ cup white wine vinegar

½ tsp sea salt

Preparation

1. Soak mustard seeds in white balsamic vinegar overnight.
2. Place mixture in blender or food processor with mustard powder, white wine vinegar, and sea salt. Process mixture to paste-like consistency.
3. Place in glass jar, cover tightly, and refrigerate for 4 days before serving.

Chef's Note: Adding your favorite fresh herbs, oven-roasted or sundried tomatoes, or oven-roasted peppers makes for exciting variations on this classic recipe.

Lacto-Fermented Cucumber Relish

Probiotic foods are an important part of the paleo diet. This cucumber relish is healthy and adds a tang to recipes and when used as a condiment.

YIELDS ABOUT 8 CUPS

Ingredients

---

4 large cucumbers, finely chopped

3 Tbsp fresh dill or 2 tsp dried dill

2 Tbsp sea salt or vegetable starter culture (follow package instructions)

Preparation

1. Mix all ingredients together in bowl. Pack tightly into sterilized quart-sized jar and place tight fitting lid on top. When packing into jar, "squeeze" out water with spoon, so that it pools on top to protect it from molding while fermenting. Add filtered, sterilized water if necessary to fully cover. Leave at least 1 inch between liquid and bottom of lid because mixture will expand during fermentation.

2. Leave the jar in warm place for 2–5 days or until completely fermented. Taste after 2 days to see if ready.

3. Once fermentation is complete, transfer to refrigerator.

{ Horseradish }

Horseradish, a member of the mustard family, is a perennial herb also related to cauliflower, radishes, and Brussels sprouts. Even though the plant grows up to 18 inches tall and 24 inches wide, it's the root that we know as horseradish.

The root is typically grated and releases a compound named isothiocyanate, which is responsible for the root's characteristic "heat." Modern preparations temper the heat with vinegar, which also adds tang. "Prepared" horseradish found in your local grocery is prepared in this modern way. Some horseradish producers are getting creative and adding vegetables, herbs, and spices to horseradish to create complex and exciting color and taste profiles.

In ancient times, horseradish was lacto-fermented like sauerkraut, yielding healthy probiotic benefits.

Lacto-fermented horseradish will last for 3–6 months in the refrigerator and maintain its healthy profile.

Horseradish roots were once difficult to find, but today well-stocked grocers and specialty or ethnic produce providers often have it in stock, especially it it's in season locally.

Horseradish is excellent when mixed with mayonnaise for an added kick to many beef, vegetable, and chicken dishes. It's also delicious added directly to many recipes or as an accompaniment to be used in moderation.

Modern Horseradish

Ingredients

1 cup horseradish root, peeled and grated

¾ cup white wine vinegar

¼ tsp sea salt

Preparation

1. Add all ingredients to blender or food processor and process until paste forms. Remove and use immediately, or store in container with tight-fitting lid in refrigerator for up to 6 months.

Beet Horseradish

Ingredients

¾ lb horseradish root, peeled and grated

1 cup red or white beets, finely chopped

¾ cup apple cider vinegar

½ tsp sea salt

Preparation

1. Add all ingredients to blender or food processor and blend until paste forms. Use immediately or store in container with tight-fitting lid in refrigerator for up to 6 months.

Lacto-Dermented Horseradish

Yields 1 cup

Ingredients

1 cup horseradish root, peeled and grated
1 packet vegetable culture starter
Filtered and sterile water
1½ tsp sea salt

Preparation

1. Combine horseradish root, vegetable culture starter, and sea salt in blender or food processor and pulse to combine ingredients.
2. Add water, one tablespoon at a time, pulsing in food processor or blender to incorporate. Add only enough water to create paste.
3. Place horseradish paste in sterilized glass jar, and add water to completely cover, leaving room for expansion. Place loose-fitting lid on top of jar. Set jar on saucer and store in warm place for 3–7 days, or until horseradish is completely fermented. Cap lid tightly and store in refrigerator for up to 6 months.

Chef's Note: If you have children, this is a great project to do with them. Use it as a teaching moment about healthy bacteria and how probiotics are an important part of a healthy digestive system. The vegetable starter used in this recipe can be acquired from a local health food store. You can also order one online. Just use the one that is easiest for you to find, fits your budget, and is suitable for fermentation of horseradish. I like to use a broad-range vegetable culture for multiple lacto-fermentation recipes.

Worcestershire Sauce

Ingredients

½ cup apple cider or balsamic vinegar

2 Tbsp water

2 Tbsp natural soy sauce (low sodium)

¼ tsp ground ginger

¼ tsp mustard powder

¼ tsp onion powder

¼ tsp garlic powder

⅛ tsp ground cinnamon

⅛ tsp freshly ground black pepper

Preparation

1. Add all ingredients to saucepan over medium heat and whisk. Gently bring to a boil, then reduce heat to low. Simmer for 15 minutes. Cool to room temperature. Transfer to container with tight-fitting lid and store in refrigerator for up to 6 months.

Worcestershire sauce is traditionally fermented, and a fermented version is healthier for you. Nevertheless, this simple recipe tastes just as good and can be made with easy-to-find ingredients.

{ Barbecue Sauce }

Paleo barbecue sauce is a little more time consuming than some other condiments because it requires the preparation of other ingredients. If this feels cumbersome, consider setting a schedule for preparing condiments on a weekly, biweekly, or monthly basis. Then, prepare the barbecue sauce at that time because you'll already have them on hand.

I like barbecue sauce because it's a nice condiment when a smoky flavor is appropriate for chicken, fish, or vegetables. Because it's paleo, there's no added sugar. Most store-bought barbecue sauces and recipes for many homemade sauces have a high concentration of added sugar in the form of brown sugar, corn syrup, granulated sugar, etc. And as we know, processed sugars aren't good for us, so try the recipe on the following page instead!

Barbecue Sauce

Ingredients

1 tsp coconut oil

1 onion, minced

1 garlic clove, minced

6 oz tomato paste

½ cup apple cider or white balsamic vinegar

½ cup water

¼ cup mild or robust ketchup (page 212–215)

3 Tbsp mustard (page 216)

1 Tbsp Worcestershire sauce (page 231)

1 pinch ground cloves

1 pinch ground cinnamon

1 Tbsp smoked paprika, add more to taste

Hot sauce to taste (optional: check ingredients to make sure it's paleo) or a few dashes of ground red pepper, to taste

Preparation

1. Heat non-stick skillet with coconut oil over medium-high heat. Add onion and sauté for 5–7 minutes or until translucent. Add garlic and sauté for 30 seconds. Immediately add remaining ingredients and reduce heat to low. Simmer for 20 minutes, stirring often, until flavors bloom.

2. Taste sauce and adjust seasonings. Increase the smoked paprika, vinegar, or hot sauce and red pepper. Stir and simmer 10 minutes longer, stirring often.

3. Remove from heat and cool to room temperature. Place in sterilized jar and cover with tight-fitting lid. Store in refrigerator for up to 30 days.

Guacamole

Ingredients

---

3 medium ripe avocados
1 firm tomato, finely diced
½ medium white onion, finely diced
½ cup cilantro, chopped
2 Tbsp fresh lemon or lime juice (more if desired)
Sea salt and freshly ground black pepper, to taste

Preparation

1. Using a knife, cut through avocado peel lengthwise, down to the seed, dividing avocado in half without pulling it apart. Using both hands, pull avocado apart. Using spoon, remove pit and discard. Spoon out flesh of avocado and place in bowl with remaining ingredients. Using fork, mash all ingredients together to form smooth or chunky texture, depending on your preference.

2. Serve immediately. If preparing guacamole ahead, press piece of plastic wrap onto surface of guacamole to minimize contact with air and resulting discoloration of avocado. Place in refrigerator until time to serve.

> **Chef's Note:** Avocados darken quickly when exposed to air. This does not affect the taste, but is unattractive. You can slow the darkening by adding a larger quantity of lemon or lime juice, or by keeping the avocado in direct contact with plastic wrap.

Salsa Verde

SERVES 4

Ingredients

½ cup onion, chopped

1½ lb green tomatillos, husks removed

⅓ cup cilantro, chopped

2 Tbsp lime juice or lemon juice

2 jalapeño peppers, seeded and chopped

Sea salt and freshly ground black pepper, to taste

Preparation

1. Cut tomatillos lengthwise and roast them either on grill or for about 6 minutes under broiler until skin is darkened.

2. Put roasted tomatillos, onion, cilantro, lemon or lime juice, and jalapeños in blender or food processor. Blend or process until smooth purée forms. Place in refrigerator to cool. Serve cool.

Chef's Note: Tomatillos are best when roasted, but simmering them in a saucepan for about 5 minutes yields good enough results for the times when you need to move more quickly.

{ Making Stock }

{ Making Stock }

Stock can be made from any animal bone, period. You can ask your butcher for bones, or get leftover one from your neighbors, co-workers, friends, and family members! Some people save bones for their animals; I save bones for my stock! Bones are very valuable when it comes to the liquid portion of most main-course recipes.

There isn't much need for precision when it comes to making stock. The most basic stock involves placing bones in cold water with a couple of tablespoons of vinegar and simmering low and slowly until a rich bouquet of flavor develops. For richer stocks, roast bones first for 25–35 minutes in a 350°–375° F oven. Then, place them in water with vinegar and simmer.

Never add salt to your stock. If you add salt now, you have less flexibility later when you are incorporating the stock into a sauce or soup that contains other savory ingredients. You can always add salt to the finished recipe, if desired.

There is no need to skim fat from stocks, unless you're making chicken stock. Chicken fat contains polyunsaturated fats that will oxidize over time and ruin the stock.

Feel free to get creative; try different ingredients in your stock. Consider using herbs and spices and combining different types of animal bones in your stock.

How long does it take?
Allow around 2 hours for fish stock, 4 hours for chicken stock, and a minimum of 6 hours for tougher bones that come from pigs, cows, deer, bison, or elk. It's virtually impossible to overcook the tougher bones. The longer they simmer, the more nutrients are extracted. I've cooked stocks for as long as 2 days. I don't usually let chicken or fish bones go more than one day because they tend to disintegrate. Remember to add water periodically to your stock to make sure it doesn't boil dry.

If you own a pressure cooker, you can make stock in under an hour! Just follow the instructions in your pressure cooker manual.

Store stock in freezer-safe containers and freeze for up to one year. Thaw before using in recipes.

Mirepoix (vegetable stock)

A mirepoix is usually a mixture of aromatic vegetables, or sometimes just the "holy trinity" of French cooking: diced carrots, celery, and onions. The French use these three in most flavoring liquids because they impart great taste and aroma (and we all know aroma is key to taste).

If adding vegetables to meat stocks, add them in the last hour or two of cooking time to avoid disintegration of the vegetables. Filter them with the bones and discard when your stock is finished cooking.

Bouquet Garni

A bouquet garni is a mixture of sturdy herbs like thyme, rosemary, and bay leaves. They are tied together or placed in a porous cloth pouch and added to stocks.

Consider adding fresh peppercorns, cinnamon sticks, or other hearty spices and herbs to your bouquet garni when making stocks.

Final Steps

Cool your finished stock in the refrigerator—not at room temperature—before final storage. Allowing stock to cool at room temperature keeps the environment perfect for harmful bacterial growth and rapid reproduction.

Once the stock has cooled completely in the fridge, ladle it into smaller containers and freeze. Only store stock you will use within 5 days in the refrigerator. If it is not used in that time frame, discard it.

Before using stock in soups, sauces, and other applications, thaw the stock and boil it for 10 minutes to kill any bacteria that may have developed during the cooling process.

{ Exercise and Paleo }

By Dustin Mohr

Dustin Mohr owns and operates "Mohr Fitness" in Johnson City, Tennessee. Dustin is an East Tennessee State University graduate and former collegiate athlete. He has helped thousands in the Tri-Cities area reach their fitness goals through the paleo diet and Crossfit style exercise. He is certified through Expert Rating Global Certifications. Mohr Fitness endorses the Crossfit philosophy, but is not an affiliate.

Over the past decade, I have seen hundreds of diets and exercise routines come and go. The diets generally last for several weeks, focusing on a very fast and intense fat loss phase. The exercise routines are usually one to two months in duration, with each day mapped out ahead of time.

Sometimes, I even see a workout plan with a diet to go along with it. These are usually pretty decent programs. Nevertheless, in these fitness magazines and on these websites, we see a different exercise program and a different diet every single month. Why is that? It's because these diet and exercise programs are focused on how much attention they can grab in a short period of time. The routines must be new, the movements must be flashy, and a new one must be introduced every month to keep the reader excited and entertained. They are fads, not lifestyles. In my experience, the only true partnership of diet and exercise that is sustainable and effective long-term is the combination of the paleo diet with Crossfit style exercise.

I own and operate a gym with a similar philosophy to that of the Crossfit franchise. The Crossfit community has really got things figured out as far as fitness goes. The approach is simple, easy to understand, and effective for the most elite young athlete to the feeblest elderly person. The name Crossfit insinuates the definition of fitness for the franchise, which is to be fit across a multitude of standards. So, by Crossfit standards, marathon runners are not the fittest people on earth because they most certainly lack strength and muscle mass. On the other hand, elite power lifters and body builders are not the fittest people on earth either, because they most certainly lack endurance and flexibility. So, a person who is "cross fit" isn't the fastest runner in the world, or the strongest person in the world, but rather a person who has balance in every area of fitness. The other area that the Crossfit community has figured out is the focus on movement rather than muscles. In most fitness magazines you will read, the exercises focus on certain body parts and working them specifically. Crossfit focuses on movements such as pushing, pulling, squatting, running, jumping, throwing, etc. Training with these movements that humans have performed for years and continue to perform on a daily basis has become known as "functional training." Rather than making a muscle bigger and aesthetically pleasing with no purpose or function, Crossfitters focus on how to enhance the performance and functionality of all the muscles involved, knowing that the growth and appearance will follow.

So, what does a Crossfit workout look like? There are a multitude of movements associated with Crossfit, ranging from weightlifting, to bodyweight movements such as pull-ups and pushups, to metabolic conditioning such as running and swimming. The reason there isn't a different Crossfit routine in popular fitness magazines every month is that the movements are combined in as many different patterns as possible. So, the routine is that there is no routine! Routine is the enemy, and with a different workout in store every day, it's impossible to plateau or become bored. The duration of Crossfit workouts also differ significantly from those of mainstream fitness magazines. All Crossfit workouts are short and intense, averaging between 15 and 30 minutes in duration. With a combination of all of these movements in an all-out burst of effort, the need to perform weight training and cardiovascular work separately is eliminated. All of your muscle building and fat loss efforts can be attained in one short workout. These anaerobic workouts are more effective than hours of aerobic work for fat loss. The answer lies in the effect of intense, anaerobic, total body training on the body's metabolism.

When a human being performs aerobic exercise, he or she burns the maximum amount of calories in the "fat burning zone." But, as soon as he or she stops exercising, the body returns to its normal metabolic rate within minutes. So, the number of calories the person burns is how many were burned from the exercise. Period. When a person performs an intense, total body, anaerobic workout, his or her heart rate and metabolism are elevated to such a high level that the body's metabolic rate will not return to normal for hours or even days. For this reason, Crossfit style workouts burn calories not only during the workout, but also for hours afterwards. This is the magic of the fat loss effect in these workouts.

It's very simple: Focusing on things that humans have done for years is the most effective style of exercise in existence. This is exactly the same approach the paleo diet takes: It eliminates unnecessary, useless ideas, and focuses instead on real, time-tested things that work for a broad range of people. For this reason, those who combine the paleo diet with the Crossfit lifestyle are among the strongest, leanest, healthiest people alive. For more information on this style of exercise and its integration with the paleo diet, visit my website www.getmohrfit.com and check out www.crossfit.com.

Make Your Own Meal Plan Template

Day	Week 1	Week 2
Mon	B: L: D:	B: L: D:
Tue	B: L: D:	B: L: D:
Wed	B: L: D:	B: L: D:
Thu	B: L: D:	B: L: D:
Fri	B: L: D:	B: L: D:
Sat	B: L: D:	B: L: D:
Sun	B: L: D:	B: L: D:

Make Your Own Meal Plan Template

Day	Week 3	Week 4
Mon	B: L: D:	B: L: D:
Tue	B: L: D:	B: L: D:
Wed	B: L: D:	B: L: D:
Thu	B: L: D:	B: L: D:
Fri	B: L: D:	B: L: D:
Sat	B: L: D:	B: L: D:
Sun	B: L: D:	B: L: D:

Make Your Own Meal Plan Template

Day	Week 1	Week 2
Mon	B: L: D:	B: L: D:
Tue	B: L: D:	B: L: D:
Wed	B: L: D:	B: L: D:
Thu	B: L: D:	B: L: D:
Fri	B: L: D:	B: L: D:
Sat	B: L: D:	B: L: D:
Sun	B: L: D:	B: L: D:

Make Your Own Meal Plan Template

Day	Week 1	Week 2
Mon	B: L: D:	B: L: D:
Tue	B: L: D:	B: L: D:
Wed	B: L: D:	B: L: D:
Thu	B: L: D:	B: L: D:
Fri	B: L: D:	B: L: D:
Sat	B: L: D:	B: L: D:
Sun	B: L: D:	B: L: D:

My Favorite Recipes

My Favorite Recipes

METRIC AND IMPERIAL CONVERSIONS

(These conversions are rounded for convenience)

Ingredient	Cups/Tablespoons/Teaspoons	Ounces	Grams/Milliliters
Almond butter	1 cup	8.8 ounces	240 grams
Coconut oil	1 tablespoon	.46 ounces	13 grams
Flour, almond	1 cup	3.4 ounces	96 grams
Flour, coconut	1 cup/1 tablespoon	4.5 ounces/0.25 ounce	112 grams/7 grams
Fruit, dried	1 cup	4 ounces	120 grams
Fruits or veggies, chopped	1 cup	5 to 7 ounces	145 to 200 grams
Fruits or veggies, pureed	1 cup	8.5 ounces	245 grams
Honey or maple syrup	1 tablespoon	.75 ounce	20 grams
Liquids: cream, water, or juice	1 cup	8 fluid ounces	240 milliliters
Peanut butter	1 cup	9 ounces	255 grams
Salt	1 teaspoon	0.2 ounces	6 grams
Spices: cinnamon, cloves, ginger, or nutmeg (ground)	1 teaspoon	0.2 ounce	5 milliliters
Vanilla extract	1 teaspoon	0.2 ounce	4 grams

Measuring Spoons	
BRITISH	**AMERICAN**
1 teaspoon	1 teaspoon
1 tablespoon	1 tablespoon
2 tablespoons	3 tablespoons
3.5 tablespoons	4 tablespoons
4 tablespoons	5 tablespoons

OVEN TEMPERATURES

Fahrenheit	Celcius	Gas Mark
225°	110°	¼
250°	120°	½
275°	140°	1
300°	150°	2
325°	160°	3
350°	180°	4
375°	190°	5
400°	200°	6
425°	220°	7
450°	230°	8